'MORE FORWARD'

by Graham Frost

This book is dedicated to John and Pauline Davoren.

John Davoren 1936 - 2008

1

Over the past few months, I have thought a lot about John Davoren, a man who played a very important part in my life. It was 1974, and I had left my family the year before. I had fallen into bad ways, and this had led me to be in trouble with the police. One day I decided that I had to separate myself from the circumstances that I was in, and after spending the night sleeping on Victoria station in London I decided to walk around the pubs in the area to see if I could get a job and a place to live. The first pub I went into didn't have any vacancies, so I tried the next one. The landlord there was Don O'Toole, and he told me that he didn't have any jobs, but he knew his friend in the pub around the corner was looking for staff, and he advised me to go and see him. That friend was John Davoren, and I went to see him. He gave me a job, and a home, on the spot. For that I am very grateful.

Not only that, but when my misdeeds caught up with me a few months later and I was whisked off to Borstal, John and his wife Pauline kept the job open for me and also came to see me while I was inside. I worked for them until 1977 and we parted company.

I recently contacted Pauline through a well-known social networking site and we spent a couple of hours chatting on Skype at the weekend. John unfortunately passed away in 2008, but I am thrilled to have had the opportunity to thank Pauline for what she and John did for me over 35 years ago. I dedicate this book to the memory of John Davoren – a very special Irishman, who had a much more difficult start in life than I did, but always tried to do right by people.

Thank you, John and Pauline.

If you haven't read my first book 'Growing Forward' there is a lot more in there about John and Pauline and how they helped me in the early 1970's when I had difficult times.

In 2013 I have met Pauline and been able to personally thank her for what she and her late husband John did for me all those years ago.

AUTHOR'S NOTE AND ACKNOWLEDGEMENTS

This book is the sequel to 'Growing Forward', my first 'autobiographical' book. 'Growing Forward' tells the story of my youth in a fundamentalist Christian cult, my escape from that organisation and how I gradually built a new life for myself. It includes a period spent in Borstal and my struggle with testicular cancer in my early twenties.

This book continues the tale. It's all true. Names and places have been changed to protect people in some cases. People told me that one of the things they liked about the first book was that it was so honest, so I have tried to do the same again.

I would like to thank Ruth Ekblom for proof-reading once again, Gary Gorman for his wonderful introduction, and Stephanie Taylor for keeping me going.

I would also like to thank my friends and supporters within Toastmasters International who kept my fire burning by asking me when the next book is out.

4

There will be a third book, and possibly even a fourth, because my life keeps taking unexpected turns, and I continue to have interesting experiences. I enjoy writing, too, once I get started!

I hope you enjoy the continuation of the story. This introduction has been updated in 2024, when I decided to 'resurrect' my writing to raise funds for Heart-Shaped Decisions CIC, my social enterprise that helps young people build confidence and self-esteem.

Graham Frost, September 2013. Edited December 2024.

I once heard a great phrase from Kriss Akabusi MBE, the legendary Great Britain athlete which went:

"The past is only for reference, not residency"

I was in the process of setting up my own business and my particular ghosts of the past were paying me a visit. They seemed to say 'You know this won't work out don't you?' 'You haven't got it in you to stick at anything....I'll give it six months and then you'll get a proper job'

And then I heard that brilliant phrase from Kriss and all my self doubts were put away firmly in the past. More precisely they were used as fuel for my future.

Graham Frost certainly has had an eventful past as anyone who has read his first book 'Growing Forward' will know. Born into a Christian cult, conquering a speech impediment, being homeless, spending a year in a young offenders institution and being diagnosed with testicular cancer at the age of 23 certainly would leave an indelible impression on any of us.

I knew nothing of this when I first met Graham at a networking meeting in 2009. I'd been the speaker at the event and Graham was kind enough to come up to me at the end and say how much he'd enjoyed my session. We got chatting and he told me about the years he spent on the railways and that he was now helping businesses deliver better customer service.

We met a few more times after that when Graham frequently came along to the breakfast networking group I ran. I nicknamed him 'my best ever audience' because he never failed to laugh at my attempted humour. To be fair, that probably says more about Graham being easily amused rather than that I have a future as a stand up comedian!

It was over the course of these next few conversations that Graham dropped in bits of his past. They seemed totally removed from the smartly dressed, professional guy in front of me. I secretly said to myself 'Blimey…I thought I'd lived an interesting life but I seem like a hermit compared to Graham.'

It can be so easy to get weighted down by our own self talk can't it? We can easily get tripped up by our own feelings of self worth, our own memories of those people who told us we'd never amount to much, our own glass ceiling. It takes a stronger character to break through and say 'You know what? I have the power of choice. And I choose to move on from the past and create my own future'. Although I've never particularly discussed it with Graham I'm guessing that this is what he has probably said to himself, maybe more than once.

If you need inspiration to move forward, to use the fuel of the past to power your future, to become the person you truly believe you deserve to be I urge you to read Graham's books. He is a beacon of hope and optimism –with a great record collection- and I'm truly grateful he's a friend.

Gary Gorman

Sales Trainer, Author & International Speaker

www.GaryGorman.co.uk

'MORE FORWARD'

by Graham Frost

Chapter One

1981 – Setting the Scene

It was 1981. I was twenty-four years of age, had made myself at home in my rented flat in Tooting and made friends with a small group of people. This had provided me with a large network of friends and I did not ever need to be alone. I had completely settled back in to my job as a steward on the railway and was accepted at King's Cross as a member of the team. I was beginning to establish a good name as a hard worker and was asked to do a lot of overtime. I rarely refused a day's work as I felt that I needed the security of having a little money behind me. It was still only just over five years since I had slept on Victoria station for the night. The memory of something like that never leaves you, and I was determined that the only way should be 'up' in my life from now on. The cancer had stayed away and I am ashamed to say that I had stopped attending the check-ups at the hospital before I had been given the 'all clear'. I simply felt so awful every time I had to go there, and was even more squeamish about needles than I had previously been, so I just stopped going for the check-ups. Fortunately for me, over thirty years later, I am still here to tell the tale.

I had not had a proper holiday since leaving home at 17 and it was time to do something about that. I went to a travel agent and picked up some brochures. I had not asked any of my friends if they wanted to come on holiday with me; the idea had not occurred to me at all. I finally decided to go on a Club 18-30 holiday in Corfu, and went back to the travel agency to book it. It was quite an exciting prospect as I had never been out of the UK before, apart from a day trip to Calais by boat a year or so earlier with my former girlfriend Anne, her husband Mark and their children. I don't know why I had gone on that trip; perhaps it was part of my recovery process after the pleurisy episode when I had nearly died.

This was a period of my life when I really wasn't sure who I was or, indeed, who I wanted to be. On the one hand, I had my railway workmates, who had mostly left school with few qualifications, like me, and would have been seen as working class – in other words, we got our hands dirty, served customers and had to work long hours in order to make a decent living. My new 'middle class' friends, however, had all been to university, or at least college, were teachers, nurses, lawyers - professional people who had opinions on world events and politics. Nick was a secondary school teacher who had moved to London from Wales. He had quite strong left-wing political opinions inherited from his father, who had been a miner. The people that I gradually started to meet through Nick were all very different from my railway colleagues, and I knew that I would be unwise to mix the two groups of friends.

The conversation in the pub after work always seemed to consist of bravado stories about real or imaginary sexual conquests, and what had gone on at work that day, while when I went out with my Tooting friends we tended to talk about slightly more cerebral matters. Not that we were boring – Nick, and I would often have the most ridiculous conversations, especially after watching the popular television comedy 'Only Fools and Horses', but he would never have dreamed of discussing what went on when he and his girlfriend were together.

My holiday to Corfu came closer and closer, and I was mightily excited. Friends couldn't understand why I was going alone, but I saw this as a challenge – I would have to talk to people I didn't know or spend a lot of time on my own. I was also still trying to discover who I really was. I had thought for a long time that I was Anne's partner, but was unable to play that role any more, so had to find another persona for myself.

I bought an entire wardrobe of new summer clothes. I hadn't worn shorts since I was a little boy, so my extremely white legs were going to get an airing for the first time in my adult life. I went to Burton's and wondered what the other lads would be wearing. I picked out several pairs of shorts, and some t-shirts, and went back to my flat and packed them in my suitcase without even trying them on. This was my holiday, and I didn't consult anyone about what I should wear or what I should do. It was to be an adventure. Would I get off with anyone on the holiday, I wondered!

I had flown before, aged 14, when my father had paid the difference between the train and plane fares and I had flown to Edinburgh for religious meetings. However, flying to Corfu was different. It was really abroad, and I had to go to the Post Office to get a British Visitors Passport. I had to go to a photo booth and have a picture taken, fill in a form at the Post Office and I immediately became the proud owner of a British Visitors Passport, valid for one year, anywhere in Europe.

The big day finally came and I made my way to Gatwick Airport on the train, and checked in at the Dan Air desk. I remember the feeling of foreboding as the plane gathered speed along the runway, and I remember the cheese roll and lukewarm coffee with powdered whitener that we were served on the flight to Corfu. People joked about Dan Air in those days as it was the forerunner of today's budget airlines. Package holidays were still a comparatively new idea and people were prepared to suffer just about any level of service just to get abroad and find some sunshine. Perhaps nothing very much has changed!

I also remember the feeling of being hit by a wave of heat as I disembarked from the plane at Corfu airport. I had definitely never been anywhere this hot. We were taken by coach to the hotel in a small town called Gouvia. I had chosen the hotel from the brochure and had opted to pay a little more to have a single room. When I arrived at the slightly up-market Park Hotel I realised that the last time I had checked into a hotel had been when my intentions were not entirely honourable. Now, I was a respectable working citizen and had paid my bill before I arrived!

The hotel was indeed very well-appointed and my room was far more luxurious than my little flat in Tooting. I had a great view of the swimming pool from my little balcony and immediately began to regret the fact that I had never learned to swim. After I had carefully unpacked the large suitcase I had brought with me for my two week sojourn in the sun, I decided to don a pair of shorts and a t-shirt and make my way down to the pool. I should mention at this point that my hair had never really grown back properly after the chemotherapy, and I had not really come to terms with that. Therefore, I was sporting what would nowadays be referred to as a comb-over. Perhaps a shy, 24-year old guy with a comb-over and a moustache is not exactly what a young lady might be looking for!

I made my way down to the pool and saw two young women who I recognised from the coach journey from the airport, swimming in the water. I bought myself a drink at the poolside bar and motioned over to them to see they would like a drink. Now, I would no more have done that at home than flown to the moon, but I was determined to try to be someone else on this holiday. I had got tired of being the quiet, sensible one and wanted to see who else I could be.

The two girls looked quite horrified, as well they might, and refused my kind offer. I saw two lads sitting by the pool with their pints of lager. I thought I recognised them from the journey too, so went over and started a conversation. It turned out that they were two mates from

Brighton who had also not fancied the regular Club 18-30 hotel down the road and had paid a little extra to stay in the better hotel.

'I've heard a lot about these 18-30 holidays,' said one, 'and my girlfriend wasn't happy about me coming really, so I thought I had better play safe.'

I immediately felt comfortable with these guys and was happy that I had decided to stay at the Park Hotel. They told me that they thought I was quite courageous to come away on my own, and that made me feel better, and accepted. I went on to spend most evenings with Tom and Ben in the bar at the Park Hotel, away from the rough and tumble of the more basic, exclusively 18-30's hotel half-a-mile or so down the road.

The two girls in the pool turned out to be quite posh and actually went through most of the holiday without talking to anyone apart from each other. One of them was really attractive but it was never possible to separate her from her friend, so I was never able to get into conversation with her. Their names were Beatrice and Ann. I remembered

17

going to school with a girl called Beatrice, and thought that she had appeared a bit stuck-up too. Thinking back, they were probably just shy, but when you are young you tend to think that if someone doesn't want to talk to you, they are 'stuck up'!

After 45 minutes sitting by the pool I noticed that the tops of my legs were beginning to smart a little. When I went back to my room I realised that I had got sunburned thighs, and had to suffer in silence for the rest of the holiday. I was ashamed to tell anyone what I had done, because I thought they would laugh at me. I had taken suntan cream with me, but thought it would be all right to sit in the sun for a short while without it. I had no idea, in those days, that after-sun lotion was available to help with the effects of sunburn. I was by no means the only young person on the holiday who overdid the sun. There were many others during the two weeks who had red body parts where they had been over-exposed to the sun. A lesson learned: when fair-skinned and abroad, always use sun cream, even if you are only outside for a few minutes.

There were many memorable experiences on that holiday. The objective of an 18-30's holiday in those days was to get rip-roaringly drunk as many times as possible in two weeks and be as outrageous as possible. For some, it appeared that going to bed with as many different people as possible was another objective, as well as not remembering anything that had happened during those drink-fuelled evenings when surfacing the next day.

A lot of the people I met on this holiday were in their late teens and early twenties, and many of them still lived at home with their parents. For some, it was their first holiday without their families, and they were really letting their hair down, literally and metaphorically. I was frankly amazed at the behaviour of some of my fellow holidaymakers, both male and female.

One morning we all had to meet up on the beach not long after breakfast and the drinking games started. I was drunk before lunchtime and learned to steer clear of the morning activities. A Greek night in a neighbouring village was memorable for the advice from our Club 18-30 representative to mix the red and white wine with orange juice 'as that will make quite a decent drink'. We were drinking this concoction from pint glasses and there were unlimited free supplies of it, so you can imagine the consequences – 100 or so drunken, uninhibited youngsters. I remember a very lovely young girl grabbing me during that evening and just kissing me passionately without saying a word. I was too drunk to know what was really going on, but I did remember her the next day and tried to follow up on the experience – she obviously had no memory of me whatsoever, so that was a non-starter!

The club representative I remember on the Corfu holiday was a burly, moustachioed character called Simon. I should not be too dismissive of people with moustaches, because I also had one at the time. Simon seemed to think that his mission in life was to sleep with as many women as possible, especially if they were on Club 18-30 holidays. Good for him, I thought, but there was really no need for him to go around bragging about his conquests for all and sundry to hear. Simon did get his comeuppance. There was a very attractive young Scottish lady staying at our hotel with her parents and brother. They were not part of the

Club 18-30 contingent, but Eleanor used to hang around with us 18-30 oiks a little during the evening, and she was very pleasant company, albeit only 17 years old.

Simon thought he was an accomplished tennis player, and he would come along to our hotel in the late afternoon to show off his prowess on the tennis court. Usually, he won, often because his opponents had been drinking since breakfast time and could barely stand up, let alone hold a tennis racquet. One day Eleanor accepted his challenge for a game of tennis, and completely wiped the floor with him. She was a very accomplished player. We didn't see Simon at the Park Hotel for the rest of the fortnight. He stayed down at the exclusively 18-30's resort half-a-mile down the road for the rest of the holiday, fortunately for us. He was one of the most annoyingly self-confident people I had ever met. What goes around definitely comes around!

All in all, my first holiday abroad was a positive experience. I had made new friends, albeit friends that I would never see again. We had exchanged contact details, but I was to learn as I went through life that it is very rare for anyone that you meet on holiday to keep in touch.

Eleanor was the exception to that rule. She did get in touch with me when she finished school and invited me to her family's large house in Scotland for a weekend a few months after the holiday. Her father was a very successful accountant and I could never understand what she saw in me, or whether she wanted me as a friend or something more. Of course, I never had the sense to ask her that question – I just tried to judge her feelings from her behaviour towards me. Yes, she was too young for me, yes, she was out of my league, but I wonder what might have happened if I hadn't been so backward in coming forward! I had a very pleasant weekend in Scotland with Eleanor. Her father was a member of one of the top Scottish golf clubs, one of the clubs where The Open Championship is played. I took Eleanor out for dinner at a lovely restaurant near where she lived, and felt totally out of my depth. Here I was, a British Rail steward who lived in a rather crummy rented flat in Tooting Bec, associating with a delightful young woman from a very respectable background in Scotland. I wonder what Eleanor's family would have said if they had known that their daughter was spending time with a former jail bird!

22

A few months later Eleanor invited herself to London to spend the weekend with me. I thought I would impress her by taking her to the theatre to see 'Blood Brothers', the Willy Russell musical that was playing in the West End with Barbara Dickson in the lead role. The only tickets I could get were for a box, so I splurged on a box for the two of us, then took her back to my flat in Tooting after a lovely dinner in a Covent Garden restaurant. I wanted something more to come of our relationship, but Eleanor was much younger than me and came from a totally different background. I was a railway steward who lived in a very ordinary rented flat in Tooting. Eleanor came from a very privileged background and I would never have been able to keep up with that. It was a great weekend and remains a pleasant memory.

After my Corfu adventure I decided that I would go away on holiday every year. It was a major step forward for me, and another milestone on the journey of escape from my restrictive family background. The following year I took another Club 18-30 holiday, this time in the resort of Lido de Jesolo in Italy. This is like Italy's version of Blackpool;

it seemed that there was nothing to do there apart from drink and party from morning until night. Luckily, Lido de Jesolo was quite close to both Venice and Verona, and I was able to visit both of these wonderful cities while on holiday. I remember seeing souvenirs priced in the millions of lira in Venice, where a cup of coffee in St Mark's Square cost me the equivalent of £6 even in those days. Verona was memorable for the great Roman amphitheatre, probably the best remaining example of such a construction in the world, and for Romeo and Juliet's balcony, which was totally surrounded by tourists, despite being a entirely fictional location, in much the same way as Platform 9 ¾ at King's Cross station is today.

Until I went on these holidays I had thought that I was a seasoned drinker, but I was discovering that I couldn't really function in the evening if I had been drinking all day, so I tried to stick to the soft drinks until about 4 pm. In Lido de Jesolo I fell in with a group of guys from the Birmingham area and had a great party with them every night for two weeks. In those days I would get home from a holiday in need of another week off to recover from the partying!

Chapter 2

Changes

Work was changing too. I had changed crews after spending a mostly enjoyable eighteen months or so working on the 10:00 Flying Scotsman. My workmates on the 10:00 had been like a little family to me .

Tommy was the Chief Steward – he was Italian and took snuff regularly, the only person I had ever met who enjoyed that habit. He was a most untidy and disorganised man and we used to joke that we needed an extra member of the crew just to tidy up after him. Alice was his right-hand woman, a very proper lady with her hair in a bun who, nevertheless, had a wicked sense of humour. Alice was married but also having a most unlikely illicit affair with Tommy, who was also married with a family. When we sat down for our staff meal they used to sit at a separate table and whisper sweet nothings to each other – it was

26

toe-curlingly embarrassing. They were both in their late forties.

Then there was Stan, the Polish chef, who used to drink with me outside of work. He was a kind man, very lonely since his wife had died a few years earlier, and he spent most of his spare time in the pubs around Clapham, where he lived. Stan's assistant was Peter, a young man from Peterborough who had married at the age of twenty and settled down with his beautiful young wife. We all went to their wedding in Peterborough – little did I know that many years later I would end up living there myself.

Bunny and Roger were the other two stewards. Bunny was Australian, gay and hilarious. He would rush through First Class on the train as we were about to go over the Scottish border and tell our American passengers to have their passports ready. Many of them would fall for the trick. Roy and I were the quieter members of the team – Roy was tall and worked hard to provide for his young wife and baby.

The cost of running a restaurant and buffet service on every train was prohibitive and the railway top brass had

27

cut down the number of staff on most of the trains, and combined the restaurant and buffet into one coach, so that there were more seats on the trains. This meant that there was the same amount of work to do, but less staff available to do it. Many of the Chief Stewards who had been enjoying a fairly quiet life and getting their hands dirty only when it was very busy found this new set of circumstances a challenge, and I had had a bit of a falling out with Tommy over the increase in my workload compared to his! I had ended up as a 'spare' member of staff. As has happened so many times in my life, this turned out to be a blessing in disguise. Being 'spare' meant that you did not have a regular train to work but had to work from week to week, covering sickness and annual leave without knowing who you would be working with or what days you would be working more than a week or two in advance.

One morning a Chief Steward who I had never met before asked me if I wanted a day's work and took me out on his train to Leeds. His name was Jack. He was very involved with the trade union, and had recently returned to working on the trains again after a spell as a full-time union official.

When we got back to London after two trips I had obviously made an impression on him, because he asked me if I wanted a regular job on his team. I wondered what he had seen that made him so impressed with me, because all that I had done was to work hard, not refuse to do anything and not stop work until everything was done. I accepted Jack's offer immediately, because I had taken to him, and I was not disappointed.

Many of the Chief Stewards on British Rail in those days were of the 'old school'. They told everyone what to do, and did very little work themselves, often sitting in the staff 'bunk' and issuing orders. Jack was different. He worked as part of the crew, took the same amount in tips as the rest of the crew, and was not frightened of getting his hands dirty. The time I spent working with Jack was some of the most enjoyable of all my twenty-four years on the railway, because he treated his team like a family, and operated on the same level as us.

I decided that if I ever became a Chief Steward I would be like Jack. I had been asked to act up as Chief Steward on one or two occasions but didn't yet feel that I was ready for the responsibility of doing the job full time.

We had the start of a great team. Jack and I worked very hard all day, somehow managing to run the restaurant and provide a coffee service throughout the train. There were two girls who worked the buffet together and our Turkish Cypriot cook, Lou, who was scrupulously clean and organised, and hated having his kitchen untidy.

Jack wasn't too happy with the performance and standards of the two girls, Ruth and Tracy so he replaced them. Although I got on well with the girls, I realised after a while that they were taking advantage of my good nature. We would work the morning train to Leeds and back, and then we would have an hour's break in King's Cross to have lunch and prepare the train for the busy afternoon trip. I would have to set up the restaurant and make sure that everything was ready for the first class service. The girls were supposed to prepare the buffet car, but what they would actually do was disappear for an hour, because they

30

knew that I would do their work as well as mine. Consequently, I wasn't getting a break at all, and I became rather fed up. I wouldn't have minded if they ever thanked me, but they just continued to take me for granted. One day I had had enough. I did all my work, went and saw the roster clerk about some overtime, and then made myself a cup of tea, sat down and drank it. When Ruth and Tracy got back on the train, ten minutes before the afternoon trip departed, they were confronted with the buffet car exactly as they had left it after the morning trip, with nothing prepared for the rest of the day. They shot me dagger looks, but they never took advantage of me again. Of course, Jack, the Chief Steward had known exactly what was going on, but he had left me to deal with it myself.

Not long after this, Ruth and Tracy were replaced by Don, a genial and experienced steward from Surrey who became a great friend of mine for several years. He did more work than Ruth and Tracey had done between them! We both had exactly the same attitude to work: we there there to work hard, enjoy ourselves and make as much money as we could. We also had Ron from Walthamstow, an ex-

31

RAF steward who was great to work with but would occasionally blow up and have to be calmed down. The last new member of the team was Hazel, who was introduced to the railway by Jack and was one of the hardest working people I ever met. Hazel started with us, and, because we all worked hard and had a laugh, she didn't know any other way. We worked a busy four-trip service from King's Cross to Leeds, starting at 7.15 am and finishing at nearly midnight, three days a week. In those days it was common for catering staff on the railway to work a 15 hour day and have the next day off. Many of us liked that system because it enabled us to work overtime on our 'rest days' which was paid at time-and-a -half. Sundays were paid at time plus ¾ so there was always a queue for Sunday working!

My new Chief Steward, Jack, only ever rebuked me once. A customer had brought back a sandwich, and complained about the quality of the bacon. In those days, all the sandwiches were made on board the train, so all I had to do was replace the sandwich. However, for some reason, I decided to be awkward – most unlike me – and refused to consider the customer's complaint. He went in search of the Chief Steward, and Jack was most uncompromising. He ordered me to give the customer another sandwich immediately, and when I had done so, he explained, quite robustly, that he never wanted to see me exhibit that kind of behaviour to a customer again. I respected Jack and apologised, and I can honestly say that I have never been rude to a customer again since that day.

Jack never spoke of this incident again, and I also learned from that. Whenever I have had to speak to someone about a work-related issue, I have had my say in private, requested the change in behaviour from the person concerned, and then the relationship returned back to normal. I try to never bear grudges in the workplace as this is energy-sapping and counter-productive. I can honestly say that it was always a pleasure to go to work when I worked with that particular team, and I probably wouldn't have stayed on the railway for as long as I did if it had not been for Jack's influence.

Soon after the bacon sandwich incident we were involved in the launch of the new Ford Sierra. The Ford Motor

Company chartered a train for six weeks to take their dealers' salesmen, representatives and mechanics to their test track in Witham, Essex, to test drive the new car. A high level of organisation was required as the journey from Liverpool Street to Witham was quite short, less than an hour, and there were 200 or more people to be served on most days. We had to serve coffee and pastries on the way to Witham in the morning, and drinks and nibbles on the return trip during the afternoon. We had some of the best staff from King's Cross on this job, and for the first time, I realised that I was quite good at this and really rather enjoyed it. We had special uniforms for the occasion, white jackets and black trousers, and I really felt that I had arrived. We would work the short trip from London to Witham, and then we had about six hours to prepare the train for the return journey. In reality, the preparation only took about an hour and a half, so we had plenty of free time. There was nowhere to go, as the train was 'stabled' in a little siding in the middle of Essex somewhere, so Don would cook us a slap-up lunch most days and we would sometimes sunbathe for a couple of hours, while being paid, of course! Fortunately, I had learned from my painful experience in Corfu and was careful not to get sunburned again. I got to know the team that worked on this job very well, as we had a lot of free time together. We called ourselves The 'A' Team, because we knew that we were the best stewards available at King's Cross. I was very proud to be included in the team and this whole episode did wonders for my self-esteem and standing within the working community at King's Cross.

Soon after the Ford Sierra launch, the Venice Simplon Orient Express was re-launched, and some of the team that I had worked with on the 'Ford job', as we called it, went to work as stewards on the Orient Express. Many people have an image of British Rail stewards in the 1980's being scruffy, sullen and very poor at customer service, but we weren't all like that.

Jack was the Chief Steward for this Ford venture too, and it meant a lot that he had selected me to be involved in this team, especially after the incident with the customer a few weeks before.

I was getting more involved in the railway social scene by this time, which might sound very glamorous, but in fact consisted of going to the pub after work most nights and drinking far too much beer. It must have been around this time that an alarm bell went off in my head one day. I was drinking alcohol, and quite a lot of it, every day, and on the very rare occasion when I didn't have a drink, I was almost totally unable to sleep. I think that state is referred to as teetering on the brink of alcoholism, and I teetered there for quite a time. Despite my better judgement, I had slipped into the habit of drinking far too much after work. When you consider that I was frequently up at 5 am, four or five days a week, and often not in bed until well after midnight, usually quite intoxicated, it was surprising that I didn't come to grief in some way.

Chapter 3

Different Friends – Different Lives

Socially, I was torn between the railway life and the middle class friends that I spent a lot of leisure time with. I was careful never to mix the two.

My musical friend and educator Mel came to a couple of the Tooting crowd parties with me but wasn't impressed. He was a bit of a loner and I understood that because there has always been a part of me that prefers to be alone. We would have our Saturday nights out together now and then, often travelling to places like Earl's Court and Richmond for a change of scene, and he left me to my own devices where my other friends were concerned. After I had known Mel for a while he told me that he could play the harmonica, and that was what had prompted his interest in the blues. Or perhaps his interest in the blues had prompted him to learn to play the harmonica. One night we went to see a local blues band at Battersea Arts Centre and Mel got up on stage with them and played a couple of numbers on his 'harp', as he called it. That led to me investigating the blues, and I was soon taking a trip to the large record stores in the West End of London, where I picked up copies of Chess Masters albums by people like Little Walter, Muddy Waters and Howlin' Wolf. Bonnie Raitt became a great favourite of mine around this time too, and I now have all her albums, either on vinyl or CD. Mel and I went to see Bonnie live at the old Town and Country Club in North London in the early 1980s – it was one of the most emotional gigs I ever went to – Bonnie is a true musical survivor and inspiration, and probably the greatest female slide guitar player of all time.

Mel would often make me compilation tapes of some of his favourite music, particularly when he was trying to 'get me into' a new genre, such as country-rock, which I never really took to. He lived in a small bedsit on Wandsworth Common, ironically just a few doors down from my former partner Anne's flat. His bedsit was very basic, and completely dominated by a massive hi-fi system and a huge record and cassette collection. I certainly modelled myself on Mel in that respect, as I have always had a reasonably good music system.

Mel wasn't too keen on some of my music, though. I was into Quincy Jones and a lot of soul and dance music, such as Earth, Wind and Fire, as well as jazz, and rhythm and blues. I remember a guitarist, who used to play a lot around the South London pub and club scene, having a conversation with Mel and me at a gig one night. Mel asked him what music he was listening to. He replied that he was listening to a lot of stuff that was produced by Quincy Jones. Mel was dumbfounded, and spent the rest of the evening saying, 'I can't believe that guy is into Quincy Jones – that stuff just doesn't do anything for me at all!'

I also tried to involve John and Cathy with the Tooting social scene but they felt that they didn't really fit in either, so I had the odd weekend with them, sometimes at my flat and other times I would go over to North London and spend a weekend with them. I suppose John was the nearest I had to a brother in those days. With most of the other people in my life I felt that I had to attain some sort of unspoken standard if I was going to be accepted by them, but with John I always felt comfortable being myself. I would sometimes spend whole weekends with John and Cathy doing very little - slobbing about, as we used to call it - and I really valued those times. Many years later I discovered that John had also had a difficult start to his life and had been adopted when he was very young.

Looking back at those times, the unspoken standard that I thought I had to attain to be accepted by people was born out of my own lack of self-esteem at the time. I was starting to be accepted at work, no mean feat in the railway industry of the time, and had also managed to forge friendships with a number of new people in a comparatively short time. I should have been feeling better about myself, but it would be a very long time before I would. Nowadays I have friends and acquaintances from all walks of life, and feel comfortable in most social situations, but the journey has been a long one!

I would often have days off in the week and tended to work at least two out of the four weekends in a month. This was because weekend working was better paid on the railway. When I had a day off during the week I would frequently go record shopping, buying the latest soul and funk records as well as getting into some jazz-funk, which was popular at the time. I had bought myself a music centre soon after moving into the Tooting flat and loved listening to music, as I still do.

I came across a British jazz-funk band called Morrissey Mullen around this time and became a bit of a groupie of theirs! I used to attend at least one gig a month in the London area, and bought their records too. They were led by guitarist Jim Mullen, who is still playing today, and Dick Morrissey, a tenor saxophonist, who unfortunately passed away a number of years ago. Their featured singer was Carol Kenyon, who would go on to have a big hit with Heaven 17; she also worked with Pink Floyd. I had a bit of a crush on Carol, and remember practically being turned into a gibbering wreck one day when the band turned up on a train I was working en route to a gig somewhere. John Critchinson, the keyboard player from Morrissey Mullen, is still playing jazz to this day, in his eighties. One day I took some of my 'university' friends to see Morrissey

Mullen, and was somewhat crestfallen when they weren't as impressed as I was. I went to see them alone after that!

I also spent hours browsing around the second-hand record stores that were plentiful in South London in those days. I could happily while away a whole afternoon doing this and found it very satisfying picking up albums for a pound or two.

After the Ford Sierra launch, I started to be offered work on the InterCity charter trains that took people to events such as the Cheltenham Festival, Grand National and York races. The passengers on these trains were avid racegoers who had paid over £100 each to go to the races for the day. We would serve a champagne breakfast on the outward trip in the morning and then dinner, often with copious amounts of alcohol, on the journey back to London. It was common for people who had made a lot of money gambling on the horses to tip us huge amounts, sometimes as much as £100 from one person, so these trips were well worth doing. It also gave me the feeling that I had joined some sort of elite, that I was being asked to take on these duties. I was accepted by my peers. It had been quite a journey, coming in as an outsider in 1979, having fifteen months off work with cancer, and then returning almost as a new starter again, but by 1983 I felt really established and had decided that I was going to stay with the railway for as long as they would have me!

Chapter 4

Alone

There was still no lady in my life. I had been on one or two dates, mainly achieved through joining Dateline, which was the pre-internet equivalent of an internet dating site, but I still hadn't met a replacement for Anne. I would think about her now and then, and wish that things had been different. I would sometimes have days of complete and abject depression, feeling very alone and not wanting to leave the flat. I usually managed to pull myself out of these feelings after a day or sometimes two, telling myself to get on with my life and be thankful for small mercies.

I did hear, two years or so after Anne and I separated, that Mark had passed away. The information came second or third hand, and I wasn't sure whether to believe it or not, but another friend of mine saw Anne in a restaurant with someone who wasn't Mark a year or two later, so that could have been true. Should I have contacted her at this point in my life and tried to rebuild something with her? Well, the decision I made was that I had to let bygones be bygones and move forward.

One Christmas, during the two years or so that I spent in the Tooting Bec flat, I spent Christmas Day alone. Sometimes friends would invite me to spend Christmas with their families, but that year I had decided that I was going to see what it was like to spend Christmas on my own. I had bought myself a small chicken and cooked that with some vegetables – my culinary skills had improved as I was now able to watch what the on-train chefs did and learn from them. I also bought myself a box of what I'm sure must have been the most horrendous white wine, probably a Liebfraumilch or Niersteiner, as that was the only wine I knew about in those days. People often ask me what it was like to spend Christmas Day alone. The answer is, it was like spending any other day alone, apart from the television, and the fact that I knew that there were people in my life who felt sorry for me, having to spend Christmas alone. The truth was that I chose, that year, to be alone, but not many of my friends would have understood that. I filled my day by watching television, listening to music, eating and drinking, just as many people do. The only difference between me and many other people was that I was alone. It didn't feel strange at all, probably because I had never been used to having a 'traditional' Christmas when I was growing up. As far as I was concerned, there were no religious connotations to the day, I had not been used to having Christmas presents, so there was nothing at all strange about spending the day on my own. I drank and ate rather a lot because I knew that was what people did on Christmas Day. I didn't really see anything strange about doing that alone. Even now, spending Christmas Day alone would not be a problem for me.

Probably because I was brought up not celebrating Christmas, I have just never got into the habit. I'm not religious, and as far as I am concerned there is no proof that Jesus was born on 25th December 0000. Over the years I have come to see Christmas as a time to get together with friends and relatives and enjoy each other's company, but it isn't obligatory. Having said that, I have had some thoroughly enjoyable Christmases at the homes of friends over the years, and am thankful to a number of my friends who really made me feel like part of their families at times when I really needed to feel part of something.

My good friend Nick, who lived in the flat below me in Louisville Road, Tooting Bec, was the first of my immediate circle of friends to meet someone that he knew he was going to marry. When I first moved into the flat, he was seeing a girl called Sarah, but the relationship was not destined to last.

One of Nick and Sarah's friends was responsible for introducing me to the music of John Coltrane. Their friend had gone to work overseas, leaving part of his record collection in Nick's care, and that was where I heard the wonderful sound of John Coltrane for the first time. It was as if I had been waiting for something for a long time, and I finally found it. I have heard and seen many jazz saxophonists since that day, but I have never heard music that made such a searing expression on my soul as that of John Coltrane. He has never been equalled as a saxophone player, in my opinion. Needless to say, I soon acquired a selection of his albums. One in particular sticks in my mind, probably for all the wrong reasons. I was in a Clapham Junction record shop called 'Nice Price Records' where I had picked up some bargains in the past. I happened upon a John Coltrane album called 'Om' in the rack and excitedly picked it up and paid 99p for it. When I got it home the music was so experimental as to be almost unlistenable, and I only ever played it once. However, I have never got rid of any of my records, even the mistakes!

Nick went away to an activity centre in Devon for a long weekend trip with some of the pupils and teachers from his school. When he came back, we went to a new 'trendy' wine bar that we had started frequenting. This wine bar was a few doors away from Marco Pierre White's first ever restaurant. I remember walking up and looking at the menu there one night. It was eye-wateringly expensive, even in those days. I noticed a change in Nick that night.. He had met someone that weekend who would change his life. Sarah was shortly to disappear from his life and the new lady in Nick's life was Karen, also a teacher, who lived quite nearby in a shared house in Norbury. Karen introduced more people into my social circle and I started to be invited to parties in two huge shared flats next door to each other in Norbury.

This was where I met Tamsin, a trainee lawyer, who was to be a great friend for many years and someone with whom I am still in contact today. Tamsin was Karen's best friend, and they still are best friends as I write this in 2013. This was the time in my life when I began to have some continuity, and realised that I couldn't keep having completely fresh starts every time I needed to make some changes in my life. Tamsin was one of the people who invited me over to her family home for Christmas. Her parents were relatively well-to-do, her mother being a retired lawyer and her father a retired senior civil servant. Tara had two younger brothers who also welcomed me into their family home. I was a little apprehensive about spending Christmas with a middle-class family, but they all made me feel extremely welcome, going out of their way to involve me in their traditional family meal and the day's festivities. I eventually relaxed and enjoyed conversations with the family.

None of the family apart from Tamsin smoked, although I was pleased that there was a fair quantity of alcohol available, so Tamsin and I had to escape every so often for a cigarette, as she smoked 'behind her parents' back'. I often wonder whether they really knew. Coincidentally, Tamsin's family lived quite near to the Royal Marsden Hospital where I had been cured of cancer just a few short years before, so it was a trip down memory lane with many different hues of mental representation for me whenever I visited their home. I had mixed feelings about Sutton, Surrey, because, on the one hand, I had been cured of cancer by the wonderful people there, but the experience of the chemotherapy had almost destroyed me at the same time.

Although I had some great friends during the 1980's, I sometimes wondered if I would ever find a new partner. Most of my friends were 'coupling up' and I definitely felt that there was something missing from my life. I would never have admitted that at the time, though, despite buying Time Out every week and scanning the lonely hearts advertisements in search of someone special.

One night Nick, another friend from Tooting called Ken, and I descended on Covent Garden where we had agreed to meet up with three young women for a triple date. Nick and Ken both had girlfriends at the time – they had done this purely as a gesture of friendship to me. It was all a bit of a flop, and the six of us had one drink together and went our separate ways.

Chapter 5

Party Fears Too!

Once again, I was stepping a little out of my comfort zone. Nick, Mark and I decided to have a party in our part of the shared house. We lived on the top three floors of the house. My small lounge on the top floor was to be the quiet place where people could sit and listen to music and chat, Nick's large room was the main hub of the party, where his superior sound system could be utilised to full effect, and we had the food in Mark's room on the next floor down. I remember Mark being quite obsessed with Tina Turner at the time, and not just in a musical way. Not very long after this party he went to live in Japan to teach English there, and I never heard from him again. Of course, in the 1980's, it was much more difficult to keep in touch with people as we had to write or telephone.

There must have been forty or fifty people at this first party, and I expanded my social circle considerably. I remember agonising over what I was going to wear. When I had attended parties before, people had tended to dress up, but I had noticed that Nick, Karen and their friends seemed to be extremely casual dressers. Nick went to work as a teacher dressed in very casual clothes with a tie around his neck, usually at half-mast and rarely matching the shirt he was wearing. In the end I wore a pair of grey Farah slacks and a blue and white striped shirt for the party, and thought I looked over-dressed and too formal. Nearly everyone else was in jeans, and I remember one girl turning up dressed in what looked like a go-go dancer's costume. A few months later I became quite good friends with this girl, and her husband, and discovered that Angela liked to dress in skimpy clothes to attract attention! Her husband, David, was a really decent guy and I often wondered how they had ended up together. At that time I was dressing like someone much older than mid-twenties!

Nick also got me into birdwatching for a short while. Birds of the feathered, flying variety were a particular passion of his, and he would take off in his car quite regularly to different parts of the country to see rare birds that had landed in the U.K. I remember one occasion when we got up at 4 am to drive all the way to Spurn Point, on Humberside, to see a particular bird that had found its way to our shores for the first time in many years. When we got there I was astonished to see there were literally hundreds of people there with telescopes and binoculars. Even before the days of the internet and mobile phones, news of this sort of thing travelled very quickly among the 'twitching' community. I also went to the North Norfolk coast birdwatching with Nick several times and fell in love with that beautiful part of the country. I still like to go walking between Holkham and Wells-next-the-Sea, a beautiful, unspoilt part of the world. Nick had a number of other friends who were much more into bird-watching than I was, although I never got to know any of them well, and I didn't become as keen a bird-watcher as Nick was, and is to this day.

Another great memory from the 1980's was attending the Capital Radio jazz festival at Knebworth Park in Hertfordshire. Unfortunately, this event took place just once, but it was to be a great experience for me. It ran over two successive weekends, and I decided to go on the two Sundays. I had decided to go on my own, because I'm quite selfish when I go to events like this and I like to go and listen to whoever I want to listen to rather than take anyone else's preferences into consideration. I remember seeing the great Lionel Hampton Big Band, with an elderly Arnett Cobb playing brilliant tenor saxophone while swaying on his crutches. The Marsalis brothers, Wynton and Branford, were also there, playing in Wynton's band. Wynton Marsalis would go on to lead the Lincoln Center Jazz Orchestra for many years, while Branford played saxophone with Sting, among others. The legendary Benny Goodman was top of the bill on the second Sunday with his clarinet and a small, young band. I remember leaving Knebworth after the second Sunday, feeling that I had been part of something really special. There was never another jazz festival in the UK with such a line-up, and to this day I feel privileged to have been there.

As I mentioned earlier, my dress sense was in need of some work, as I tended to dress like a 40-year old, shopping for clothes at Burton's and not being very adventurous. In my defence, I had to wear a uniform at work, and Anne had liked me in shirts and slacks, so my sartorial education had been rather half-hearted.

Fortunately, help was not too far away. One of the new friends I had made was Tom, an East Ender who had trained as an artist and lived in Crystal Palace with a gorgeous Liverpudlian hairdresser called Jo. I would often go over to their flat on my day off to listen to Tom's extensive collection of jazz and other excellent music, and, let's be frank, to smoke dope!

This was where I heard Captain Beefheart for the first time and Tom also introduced me to the music of Tom Waits. I had got into Quincy Jones through listening to the radio so my musical tastes were becoming very wide-ranging. I remember going to see Tom Waits at Hammersmith Odeon around that time – he played a harmonium just like the one my grandparents had in their front room when I was a little boy. To this day, if anyone asks me what my favourite album is, I always answer, 'The soundtrack to 'One From The Heart' with Tom Waits and Crystal Gayle.' An unlikely combination of singers, but one that works, and I have Tom to thank for that. I was also an avid reader of the New Musical Express in the eighties and would often buy albums purely on the recommendation of some of their critics. I particularly enjoyed the writings of Richard Cook in the NME. They used to cover such a wide range of music in those days, and my musical tastes today are a result of the people I knew in the 1980's and the NME.

Tom's girl friend, Jo, introduced me to some friends of hers who had a second-hand clothes stall on the new Covent Garden market. They would trawl around jumble sales all over South London, buying second-hand clothes, then tidy them up and sell them at a profit at Covent Garden, which had just been refurbished and launched as a major shopping and tourist destination, after having been a fruit and vegetable market for many years.

I went to Fred and Desiree's house in Sydenham with Jo. Fred was German and Desiree was of Polish origin. They had a huge room in their very impressive three-storey house full of their stock and I was able to select anything I wanted and pay a reduced rate for it. I was reminded of the time when I was 14 and my mother had bought me second hand clothes, but there was no denying that I looked much better in the second hand tweed overcoat, drainpipe trousers and collarless shirts than I did in my usual Burton's gear!

Jo also encouraged me to cut off my comb-over. I had caught sight of my reflection in a shop window during a high wind a few days earlier and had taken to wearing a hat most of the time, but Jo convinced me that there was nothing wrong with being bald at the age of 27, and I am very glad that she did. Jo was extremely sexy and reminded me quite a lot of Anne, but I was not prepared to get myself into another mess by trying to make a pass at someone else's partner again, so I kept my feelings to myself. I have often wondered why people that I can't or shouldn't be with are often more attractive than those I can!

Tom was a very interesting character. Born in the East End of London, he was part of a large family but had very little to do with them. He had been to art school and sometimes earned a living as a teacher, but was quite often out of work while his long-suffering girlfriend worked as a hairdresser in Croydon. One of the things that sticks in my mind about Tom was the burning bush 'sculpture' made out of crisp packets that he had in his back garden. We remained friends for several years, but after Jo finally tired of him and moved out he became increasingly eccentric and we lost touch.

A few weeks after my visit to Fred and Desiree's house, they invited me to dinner. I was asked to bring a bottle of Verdiccio wine with me. It was a good thing that they suggested what wine I should bring, as I had no idea about wine at all in those days, despite working in the catering business. They had invited a female singer round for dinner too. She turned out to be a charming woman, who had a hit single a year or two later, and is still active as a jazz singer. I wonder if she still remembers the night she had dinner with the shy guy who was somewhat in awe of her.

Chapter 6

Broadening Horizons

Another friend I made during the Tooting days was Chris, an advertising executive whom I met in The Windmill pub on Clapham Common. The Windmill was a regular watering hole of mine and it was almost impossible to go in there without meeting someone that I knew. I still used to meet old Stan, the Polish railway chef, in there sometimes, but this particular evening I was standing at the bar with a pint of Young's ordinary bitter, smoking a cigarette, and probably either staring into space or people-watching, always one of my favourite occupations. A skinny, bearded guy came up to me and asked me for a light. We got into conversation, and it transpired that he lived at the other side of Tooting Bec Common from me. We chatted for a while and he said he was recently separated from his second wife and would I fancy going for a pint or two with him now and then.

I agreed, and we struck up a friendship that lasted for several years. We would sometimes meet for lunch in the Coach and Horses in Soho, the pub immortalised in the play 'Jeffrey Bernard is Unwell', and I was regularly served by Norman Balon, who was widely known as London's rudest landlord. I thought the Coach and Horses was a great pub and also started reading Private Eye, as the editor and staff of that magazine were regulars in the Coach and Horses. Chris drove a VW Golf GTI, quite a sought-after car in those days, and we would often drive over to Chelsea or Richmond in it to have a beer or two.

I felt myself to be incredibly fortunate to have Chris as a friend. He was a member of Middlesex County Cricket Club and could get Test Match tickets, often at reduced prices. We were both huge cricket fans, and I can remember several days spent at Lord's with Chris, revelling in the great West Indies team of the time or watching the Australian bowlers, Lillee and Thomson, giving the English batsmen a good roughing up with their fast bowling. Cricket has played a massive part in my life since I got into watching the game on television when I was suffering with cancer. During the 1980s there was a train driver's strike, which meant that the staff who were not on strike got paid just for going into work and signing in. That gave me the opportunity to go to two complete Test matches, all five days, one summer. There is nothing like a day at the cricket and I still go to London at least once a year for a day at a Test match.

We would also go to see Fulham play football now and then, although we stopped going when there was crowd trouble during a Fulham v Chelsea match at Craven Cottage and I saw people behaving more violently than I had ever seen in my life. As far as I'm concerned sport is to be enjoyed. I have no objection to people enjoying a few drinks, because I do myself, but there was no excuse for what I saw that day, and it was many years before I went to another big football match.

Eventually, Chris met a girl from his office who was a good deal younger than him, gave up smoking, became a part-time vegetarian and got married for the third time. I bought tickets for him, Rebecca, his new girlfriend, and me to see Miles Davis at Hammersmith Odeon in 1982, and ended up selling two of them to a ticket tout outside the theatre as Chris and Rebecca were unable to make it at the last minute. I sat enthralled as Miles Davis and his band played electric jazz for two hours. This was the only time I ever bought a live album on my way into a concert. It is called 'We Want Miles' and I still play it regularly to this day.

I went to Chris and Rebecca's wedding in Bognor Regis, where her family came from, but our friendship petered out shortly after the wedding. I did meet Chris once or twice more for lunch at The Coach and Horses in Soho. He would have sausages and mash as he told me his new wife had almost turned him vegetarian and made him give up cigarettes and coffee.

Quite early in 1984, the elderly landlord of the house in Louisville Road let it be known that he was selling the house and that we would all have to move out. By this time there was Nick and me, a rather eccentric guy who drank a lot and drove an American car, a professional musician and a drug dealer (well, we thought that was what he did) living in the house.

I was approaching 28 years of age and thought that if I was going to have to move, it was going to be into a home of my own. I started thinking about buying a flat, instead of renting again, and began looking around in the Tooting and Balham area. Unfortunately, even in 1984, property prices were comparatively expensive in that part of London and nearby Clapham had already become very gentrified. I went to the building society to see what I could borrow in the way of a mortgage.

The manager looked at me sternly over his desk.

'Mr. Frost,' he said, 'We would be much more likely to offer you a mortgage if you had another thousand pounds in savings – if you can do that we will be able to lend you twenty-two thousand pounds'

The prices of one-bedroom flats around where I wanted to live were in excess of £25,000, so I knew that I would have to look further afield. Where was I going to get another thousand pounds from? The idea of giving up on my dream of home ownership did not occur to me. I hadn't survived everything that had been thrown at me for the last few years by giving up. I would go back to the drawing board, although I wasn't sure how!

Thankfully, British Rail came to the rescue. The very next day I went into work where I heard that a large American air conditioning company were bringing hundreds of their employees to the U.K. for a whistle-stop tour by train. They would be arriving at Heathrow, spending two days in London, travelling by train from London to York, where they would spend three hours, then continuing to Edinburgh by train, where they would spend a day before flying back to the United States direct from Scotland. A crew was needed for a charter train operating three days a week for six weeks. Was I prepared to work the charter train on my days off while continuing to work my regular shift?

You bet I was! In those days there was a continuous duty payment for staff who had less than a certain number of hours break between shifts. If I worked these charter trains and my own shifts I would be paid continuously 24 hours, Monday to Friday, for six weeks. Then I had my weekends to work as well. It was extremely tiring and challenging. I was put in charge of serving 120, or more, demanding American customers several times, but I managed to get through the six weeks without losing my mind.

We had a chef on that job who had very poor eyesight and very little idea of how to cook. In those days, being able to cook was not a pre-requisite of getting a job as a chef on the railway! One day I had the misfortune to have him as my chef. There were two other members of staff, plus myself, to serve 120 Americans a full English breakfast, with all the trimmings, silver service, in ninety minutes. Chas's idea of cooking bacon was to take it out of the packet and slap it on a cooking tray under the grill for a few moments before arranging it untidily on a serving tray, with sausages, tomatoes, fried bread and fried eggs. The bacon was piled on to the serving tray, and I realised very quickly that the bacon at the top was burned, and the bacon underneath was raw. The sausages were burned on one side and raw on the other, and I won't go into the situation with the eggs – they were like rubber. I had no option but to serve this awful food to the customers as there wasn't anything else. Fortunately, they were only on the train for short time, and I think many of them had already had breakfast in their hotel, but I can understand how British Rail came to have a name for dreadful food in the 1970's and 80's.

At the end of six weeks hard labour I had the deposit I needed to buy my first flat. I went along to see the manager of the building society again, and he was staggered that I had managed to raise another £1,000 so quickly. To be honest, so was I, to say nothing of being shattered from working practically seven days a week for four weeks and spending at least three nights a week sleeping on trains. I would literally finish a 12-hour shift on my own train, which was two trips from London to Leeds and back, go to the sidings, help to prepare the charter train for the next morning and then grab a few hours sleep before spending most of the next day serving a train full of Americans. Our charter train would go back to London empty overnight, which provided the opportunity for a reasonable night's sleep, then I would go off to Leeds again and repeat the cycle.

The building society would now lend me £20,000, so I had around £22,000 to spend on a flat. The only area where I could get a proper self-contained flat for that price was Brixton, or the surrounding areas. When I mentioned to friends that I was thinking of buying a flat in Brixton, there were a few raised eyebrows. Brixton was a predominantly black area, and there had been trouble there in the past. A lot of my friends also thought I was a little crazy wanting to buy a flat in the first place. I had gone through a socialist phase when I thought that property was theft for a while, but the pragmatist in me didn't see the point of paying rent to a landlord and making them rich for the rest of my life. I thought I could be a property-owning socialist and still be true to my beliefs.

Chapter 7

My Own Home

I ended up buying the first flat that I viewed. It was a ground floor conversion just off Brixton Hill, quite near to Brixton prison. There was a lounge, bedroom, kitchen diner and bathroom, and I had half the back yard! The flat I was moving out of was furnished, so I had to buy furniture too. I remember going to Habitat in Tottenham Court Road to buy some of the furniture, using my newly-acquired Access card. Buying the flat had completely cleaned me out financially and I knew that I was going to have to work hard over the next few months to get some money behind me again.

I was the first tenant to move out of the house in Louisville Road, and I had moved so quickly that I didn't get the financial bonus from the landlord for moving. He ended up offering a reward to the other tenants to move out once he had sold the house. I knew that I would miss the camaraderie of the house in Tooting with its shared public phone and the very cheap rent and utilities. The gas and electricity meters had not been recalibrated for years and 50p lasted a week in my electricity meter! The central heating was also included in the rent, and if we wanted it hotter, we just went and turned it up. We were so innocent in the days before concerns about global warming!

I moved into my flat in Brading Road, Upper Tulse Hill, in November of 1984. Another new start for me, another step on my journey. I remember the Saturday night after I moved in, inviting all my Tooting and Norbury friends to a house warming party. One by one, they all rang to say that they couldn't make it. I was very disappointed and thought that because I had moved away they were going to lose touch with me. I was sitting in the flat feeling quite sorry for myself when the phone rang. I was now the proud owner of my own direct phone line for the first time!

Tamsin, a great friend, was on the phone. She told me that she had been meeting someone in the Telegraph pub in Brixton Hill and they hadn't shown up. Was it all right if she popped round for a cup of tea? I agreed readily, thinking that at least I wouldn't have to spend the evening alone and wondering what had possessed her to agree to meet someone on her own in a pub in that area!

Tamsin came around, and then gradually one by one, two by two, all the friends that I had invited turned up, bringing food and drink. It turned out that they had all received the posted invitations and decided to play a trick on me by refusing the invitation. I don't think any of those people knew at the time how important they were to me, and what a difference having them as friends made to my life. I have lost touch with the vast majority of them now, but that was a very special evening for me. I accept that friends come and go in life, but there are some that have been there at special times that I will always remember. I ended up with about fifteen people in the flat that night and had to go out and buy fresh supplies of food and drink – that was a measure of the success of the evening! I am happy to say that some of those fifteen people are still friends to this day. The sort of people that you might not see for years, then carry on conversations that started thirty years ago, with everyone knowing exactly what you mean.

Soon after moving into the flat in Brading Road I bought my first video recorder. Up until that point I had rented a video machine from Radio Rentals, but I became the proud owner of my own VCR in early 1985. It cost £400, which was a fortune in those days, but a video recorder was an essential piece of equipment for the railway worker who worked very unsocial hours. When I had a day off I would often spend the whole day catching up with my favourite television shows. These included Brookside, the fashionable (at the time) Channel 4 soap opera that starred Ricky Tomlinson and Sue Johnston, who would, many years later, go on to work together on The Royle Family. Many of the early episodes of Brookside were written by Jimmy McGovern, who would go on to find fame and success as the writer of 'Cracker'. I also have to admit to having been addicted to Dallas and Dynasty at the time, so my days off were often spent immersed in a fantasy world of television soaps!

One of the routines that became established in my life around that time was going to The Cricketers at The Oval at lunchtime on the Sundays when I was not working. The

Cricketers was a music pub that put on very high quality r'n'b, soul and blues bands on Sunday afternoons. In those days, the pubs were open from midday until 2 pm, so there was an almighty rush to get as much beer drunk in two hours as possible. I would meet up with my friend Mel there. In fact there was a small crowd of us, about four or five strong, that would get together quite regularly. One of the bands that played there quite regularly was Snake Davis and the Suspicions. Snake Davis was the saxophone player who went on to fame a few years later with M People, but this band played excellent covers of soul and r'n'b originals such as Junior Walker & The All Stars. It was fabulous music and The Cricketers would be packed solid on most Sunday afternoons. I remember the Snake Davis band had a Hammond organ player who used Leslie speakers – the first time I had heard an organ played like that – it was very stirring. Leslie speakers revolve very fast when they are switched on and produce a unique swirling organ sound.

We would often follow a session at The Cricketers with Sunday lunch at Battersea Arts Centre, a bus ride away, and then go back to someone's flat for music and sometimes a Sunday afternoon nap, depending on how much alcohol had been consumed during the afternoon! Sometimes I would make my way across the road to The Oval cricket ground to watch a Sunday league limited-overs cricket match and have lunch from the burger van there instead.

By now I was becoming quite well known at King's Cross for being good at my job, and a reliable member of staff. It had taken a long time to be accepted, but I had now been working on the railway for over five years and had no thoughts of moving on to work anywhere else. I had weathered the initial storms and was earning good money. With overtime and tips, I was at least as well off as most of my friends, and better off than some of them. I remember having a conversation with Tamsin, my friend who was a trainee solicitor, and at the time, earning a lot less than I was. I told her that ten years from then, I would probably be earning a lot less than she was, because my opportunities were limited because of my comparative lack of education. I was proved right; many years later Tamsin was earning two or three times as much as I was!

My unofficial mentor, Jack, had gone back to a full-time position within the trade union. He was to stay with the union for many years. I belonged to the railway staff union for the whole of my railway career, but was never involved beyond being a member and paying my dues. It seemed to me that most of the people involved in the union at that time, with the exception of Jack, were purely involved for their own benefit, and not really interested in what they could do to help their colleagues. This was a pity as I believe in trade unions as a way of keeping workplaces fair for employees.

When Jack went back to work for the union he was replaced by another Chief Steward, Del, who was from North London and a fellow Tottenham Hotspur supporter. I am probably the only Tottenham supporter in the world who has only ever been to two or three games in my entire life, but I had decided that I was a Tottenham supporter when I was at school in Colchester, when Jimmy Greaves played for the Spurs.

It was a little different working with Del. He would usually turn up quite late for the train and expect the rest of us to be there on time and to have prepared the train in his absence. Eager to please our new Chief Steward, we adapted, but there was a bit of internal unrest within the team when we realised that we were being expected to work harder for less tips. Del was much less democratic than Jack had been, and it wasn't such a pleasant working environment. We realised how fortunate we had been to have had Jack as our Chief Steward for the past year, and Don from Sussex and I, who had become very good mates, decided that we had to speak to Del about how things were going. We had a brief chat in the pub with Del over a few pints one night, and things did change for the better. He started sharing out the tips more fairly and getting his hands dirty a little more often. However, I would have to say that when thinking about the leadership qualities of the two Chief Stewards, Jack would always come out on top, because of his inclusive style and the fact that he was very much part of the team and never asked anyone to do something that he wouldn't do himself.

We had moved to the 07.50 train from King's Cross to Leeds, which still involved two trips in each direction from London to Leeds, with the 07.50 being a business express service on which we would regularly serve over seventy full English breakfasts, silver service, freshly cooked on board the train, as well as a busy buffet car with hot food and drinks. Fortunately, we had an excellent team and no-one was afraid of getting their hands dirty, or wet, as we had to do all the washing up on board the train too, by hand, in those days! This was where I learned about teamwork and communication – if there was something that needed doing, you just got on and did it, it was rare that anyone had to issue an instruction.

Chapter 8

Riots and more change

I think that the whole Anne episode had completely wiped me out as far as women were concerned. I had gone back to the person I had been before I was with her, and had no confidence at all that I would be any good to anyone. As for chatting women up on holiday or in bars at home, that is something I have rarely been able to do.

I had been living in Brixton, or as I described it, Upper Tulse Hill, for under a year when the second round of Brixton riots kicked off. I had started referring to my address as Upper Tulse Hill because the road I lived in was, in fact, off Upper Tulse Hill, but also because I had become tired of some people asking me how I could live in Brixton. The answer was, 'Easily,' because I did not for one moment ever feel out of place there. I got on well with my neighbours and occasionally went to the very multicultural local pub too.

I had been working a long 14-hour shift on the night the 1985 Brixton riots kicked off. I arrived back into King's Cross from Scotland, completely unaware of what was happening in Brixton, had a couple of pints in the pub with one or two work mates and went to get the tube home. It was, for me, a normal evening. I noticed a sign on the Victoria Line platform saying that the Victoria Line trains were terminating at Stockwell. There was no further information. I mentally shrugged my shoulders and decided to get a bus home from Stockwell. By the time the train reached Victoria, the trains were terminating there, well short of Stockwell. I was slightly frustrated as I was due to be working overtime the next day and needed to get to bed but this was making me late. I was still in the dark about why the trains were terminating so short of their destination. However, I decided to get a train from Victoria to Streatham Hill and then walk home or catch a bus down to Brixton Hill. By the time I got off the train at Streatham Hill I knew something was wrong. There was menace in the air, tangible and unexpected; I could smell burning, hear sirens and see smoke rising.

When I walked to Christchurch Road there was a barricade across the top of Brixton Hill, manned by police. As I walked through, a policeman called out to me,

'I wouldn't go down there mate.'

I replied that I had to and carried on. There had been riots in Brixton before, in 1981, when I had lived in Tooting, and I wasn't going to let a few rioters scare me. My feelings changed when I got nearer home and saw a bunch of guys looking as if they were trying to set fire to the petrol station just a few hundred yards from my home. My pace quickened, my heart started beating a little faster, I was caught between wanting to watch what they were up to and not wanting to, and I reached the safety of my flat a few moments later. It was quite a relief to get there in one piece.

I went and put the kettle on, then realised that I was hungry, and, true to form, had no food in the house. I had noticed, as I came close to my flat, that my local fish and chip shop was closed, but the Chinese take-away out on Brixton Hill was still open, so made my way back out for some food. In those days, we were well fed at work, so I didn't need a lot of food in the fridge at home, as I worked at least five days out of every seven. I mentally told myself off for being so disorganised with my shopping, but figured that if I had made it home safely once, I should make it a second time. Things appeared to have quietened down a little in the few minutes since I had arrived home, but I was the only customer in the Chinese take-away and they expressed surprise that I was out and about. I told them that I was surprised, but very pleased, to see that they were open.

Arriving home, I settled down to watch the events that were happening just a mile from my home unfold on the BBC television news, hoping that the rioters wouldn't creep any further up Brixton Hill. The next morning I caught the bus down to Brixton to go to work and noticed the smashed windows and burned out shops in Brixton town centre. It was impossible to miss the broken windows and smell of burning. There was just the one night of serious rioting, and my own life was completely unaffected, apart from the one disrupted journey home

81

from work, but, it was many months before Brixton got back to its colourful, lively self again.

In the mid-to-late 1980s there were quite a lot of changes on the railway. We didn't know it at the time, but we were being prepared for privatisation, and there was a lot of unrest. We started selling food products that were prepared off the trains, such as the infamous bacon and tomato rolls that were supposed to be cooked in the microwave. I had always taken a great pride in the sandwiches that I made and sold on the trains – my 'quality control' was my own – I worked on the principle that I would sell a customer a product that I would be happy to buy myself. Unfortunately, not everyone on the railway worked that way, and the new senior managers wanted to create a consistent product, so we had to sell a consistently poor product because that was easier than trying to manage people to do their jobs properly. That was how I saw it, anyway. It was said that Prime Minister Margaret Thatcher hated the railways, and was determined to make them more efficient. Whether or not that was true, I do know that she only ever travelled by train twice during her entire time in office.

It wasn't as much fun going to work anymore, there was more pressure, and I knew that some new crews had been created just to work charter and land cruise trains throughout the year. A year or two before, I had applied for a job on the Orient Express, which was staffed by ex-British Rail stewards, but I had been unsuccessful.

The InterCity charter train unit was set up in the 1980s to run so-called land cruises and offer corporate train charters, as well as specialised excursions aimed at what we used to refer to as train-spotters. They prefer to be known as railway enthusiasts. The coaches that were used for these trains were all Mark 2 coaching stock. This meant that they were all 1940s and 1950s built carriages, without air conditioning; there was also some asbestos used in their construction. Additionally, there were some Mark 3 air conditioned coaches, and the original 1960s Manchester Pullman set of coaches were used as well. There was an organisation called SLOA – short for Steam Locomotive Operator's Association which owned a set of 1950s

83

Pullman coaches and these were also in frequent use, often with steam engines hauling the trains for all or part of the journey. A perennial favourite train with railway enthusiasts was *The Pennine*. This ran every Wednesday from May to October and went from King's Cross to Leeds, sometimes stopping to pick up more passengers en route. It stopped at Leeds and had a steam engine attached for the journey from Leeds to Carlisle via the Settle to Carlisle line, one of the most scenic railway journeys in the world. The train would complete its journey, diesel-hauled, from Carlisle to London Euston via the West Coast main line. Other popular trips were the weekend 'land cruises' from London to Inverness or Fort William, and there were eventually land cruises to Penzance and the Isles of Scilly as well as to Wales and the West. These trains would take over 100 passengers on three or four day excursions with one or two nights in sleeping cars and one night in a hotel. The journeys consisted of eating and drinking while looking out of the train window, and often listening to a running commentary on places of interest as the train was passing the landmarks. Visits to interesting destinations such as the Glenfiddich whisky distillery in Dufftown were included in the itinerary, and the cost of the weekend trips, including all meals, but not drinks, was in the range of £300 per person. Many of the passengers were quite well-off retired and business people who liked to relax completely for the weekend and enjoy being waited on hand and foot! The tips could be excellent too, according to one or two of my colleagues who had already worked on the charter trains.

I decided to make myself available to work charter trains on my weekends off, and see if I could get myself a regular job there. I knew some of the staff quite well, as they had previously worked at King's Cross, and I had worked the Scottish charter train with them when I had been saving for the deposit on my flat.

The land cruise trains went to the Highlands of Scotland every weekend, leaving London on a Friday night and returning on Sunday night or Monday morning. I couldn't really work these as it would have interfered with my usual roster, but I made myself available for the one-day excursion trains, where we would serve over 120 silver service breakfasts, lunches and dinners to the same people during the course of a long, arduous day. It was much more enjoyable work than selling pre-packed sandwiches and microwaved snacks to largely unappreciative customers on the main line, and I felt happier at work again, although I was only working the excursion trips for odd days here and there. I was using my customer service skills and the tips were better too! I think it was because the passengers on the charter trains, by and large, wanted to be there, whereas those on the main line trains often had to be there. There is a subtle but real difference!

Eventually, after several months of combining the two roles, one of the older stewards who worked on the charter trains decided that he really couldn't handle the hours any more, and I was offered a permanent job on the charter crew. I was very pleased, although it did mean leaving Dom and Hazel, and the rest of the team that I had enjoyed working with for quite some time. Eric, the charter crew Chief Steward, offered me the opportunity to work with him full time at the end of a Saturday trip to Yorkshire, and I accepted straight away, although I said that I would have to be officially 'released' from my current job by the management at King's Cross. This took place within two weeks, and I officially became part of the charter crew. In some ways, it was like going back to my early working days on the railway, because the trains we used were very old, and the kitchen cars were of the gas-fired variety having been built in the 1940s and 50s. They were, however, better maintained and generally things worked quite well.

Some of the staff I teamed up with on the charter trains were also reminiscent of the old boys that I had worked with in 1979 when I first joined British Rail. They were reaching the end of their careers and some of them should not really have been working so hard or such long hours at their time of life. There was poor old Barry, who suffered from severe arthritis and took about half-an-hour to get moving in the morning. He was one of those people who thought he was funny and would constantly crack the same, unfunny jokes, and then laugh at himself. Despite that, there was no harm in him, but he wasn't really the sort of person you wanted on your team when you were trying to serve 120 breakfasts, silver service, in an hour and a half. Tom was another old steward who had been around for years, drank quite a lot and thought he was a comedian too. Unfortunately, he also thought he could get away with doing little work, and always seemed to be missing when there were huge piles of washing up to be done. There was, however, a very hard-working girl called Jayne on the crew and she and I, together with another guy called Chas, did most of the work, or so it seemed to us. The crew was completed by Lenny, who thought he was working on a cruise liner, or that was what we said, because he loved having his picture taken by the passengers, was always immaculate, and shied away from any really hard work. We called him The Poser. Chas and I became great mates and worked well together as well as rooming together whenever we were away from home. We remained friends for several years. Finally, there was Eric, the Chief Steward, who was a very nice man but was unable to stand up to anyone on the crew. I knew Eric from my time on the American charter train in 1984 when I had saved the deposit for my flat in six weeks, and we respected each other. The kitchen staff were Bert, who I had known for many years, and a variety of kitchen assistants came and went, as Bert could be difficult to work with.

On the charter trains we never had a weekend off. We would work excursion trains every Saturday, and most Wednesdays. During the summer tourist season, we would be lucky to get one day off a week. I threw myself in to this new lifestyle with some gusto, delighted that I was no longer serving warmed up bacon and tomato rolls and poor-quality pre-packed sandwiches. I had the opportunity, once again, to put something of myself into my work.

The money was terrific although there was little time to spend it. We were fed and watered at work and some weeks would be at home for only one night. I became an expert at getting to sleep in a sleeping bag in an old railway compartment – they could be very comfortable, particularly when you had worked three fifteen-hour days one after the other! I was so busy working that I had little time to think about all the things that I had run away from over the past ten years or so. I didn't want to think about my family, I didn't want to think about Anne and I didn't want to think about the fact that I was living alone.

Although I enjoyed the job very much and was making a great living, I rarely had time to think about anything other than the next trip.

A typical week on the charter trains, in the height of the summer season, would involve arriving back from a West Highlander trip to Oban and Fort William at 8.00 on a Monday morning, having been away since Friday. We would have to return our stock to the catering stores at St. Pancras before going home. Some of the team would go to a pub in Farringdon, near King's Cross, that opened all day, but I could never drink in the morning, so would go home, put some washing in the machine and go out to the nearby Co-op supermarket to buy some food. Or I might go to a cafe and have some breakfast, after taking a bath. The rest of Monday I would relax and watch television programmes that I had recorded over the past week or two. Monday was a quiet evening and an early night.

Tuesday morning I would start preparing uniforms for the rest of the week. We had white jackets and shirts that had to be ironed, six or seven of each. It was possible to get the white jackets laundered at work, but you never got the same ones back from the laundry, so we all laundered our own. By lunchtime on Tuesday I would often be at King's Cross, ready to load the supplies on the train for our Wednesday steam train to the Pennines trip. Three or four of us would load all the food and drink to serve 250 customers for breakfast, lunch and dinner into a van, which would then be driven to Bounds Green sidings in North London by Ernest, our lovely, good-humoured West Indian driver. We would then unload the stores onto barrows and push or pull the barrows into the sheds where the trains were kept and prepared. Our next job was to physically lift all the boxes and bags of food and drink onto the train, and stow it all away in the kitchen vehicle. Them, often after a cup of tea, we would lay the coaches up for breakfast, and prepare all the china and glassware for the next day. By the time we had completed all these tasks it would often be between 8.00 and 9.00 pm. The chef would provide us with a bite to eat, or we would go to the nearby pub for a couple of pints, sometimes stopping off for fish and chips on the way back, if the chef hadn't had time to feed us. He would have been busy preparing for breakfast, lunch and dinner for over 100 customers the next day.

We would sleep in old First Class compartments usually. It helped to be really tired, or slightly drunk, as it was difficult to sleep in train maintenance sheds where the main line trains were being worked on overnight. There was always a lot of hammering and drilling going on. You did well to get two or three hours sleep. We told ourselves that we were being paid for sleeping, which was true, but I remember many nights of tossing and turning, just getting off to sleep and then being woken by a loud noise from some nearby maintenance work.

We would be up and working again by just after 5 am. There were always two catering crews and two kitchens on each train. As soon as we got up, we would start preparing for breakfast. The only way to serve 125 full English breakfasts, silver service, with starters and toast, unlimited tea and coffee, in an hour and a half, is to be totally prepared. By the time our passengers and the rest of the crew joined us at 7.30 am, in King's Cross or Euston station, we would be ready, resplendent in our uniforms, having had a rather unsatisfactory wash and shave in one of the train toilets.

We would greet our passengers as they boarded the train. Many of them were regular travellers, often retired people who enjoyed a trip down memory lane on the trains of the 1950's and 60's. They were, by and large, pleasant and easy to serve, and appreciative. Quite the opposite of a lot of the passengers on the main line trains. This was what made the job enjoyable, and made all the preparation time worthwhile – the opportunity to do a really good job and be appreciated for it.

We would serve breakfast, clear down all the tables and wash up after our 125 people, then it was almost immediately time to start preparing for lunch, which the passengers would eat just before they got off the train for an hour at one of the stations in the Pennines. If we were fortunate, we had time for a bacon sandwich while we were washing up. Lunch, for the passenger, usually consisted of soup and sandwiches, which were served at their tables, together with soft or alcoholic drinks, which had to be paid for. All the food was included in the price of the trip. We had to time the service strictly so that we were not still serving when the train arrived at the station where the passengers were getting off to stretch their legs for an hour.

During the hour that the passengers were off the train, we had to re-lay all the tables for dinner, including glasses and folded linen napkins, and help the kitchen team of two to prepare cold starters. We also had to make sure that all our main course plates were clean and in the hot cupboard. Very much like what goes on in the banqueting department of a large hotel, but often while travelling at up to 100 mph. We considered ourselves very fortunate indeed if we got to have a break during one of these one-day excursions. In fact, we used to joke that we wouldn't sit down if we did get time, because we might not get up again! Having said that, there was plenty of good humoured banter among the crew and we were all mostly pulling in the same direction!

We would arrive back into London, having served our customers a three-course dinner with drinks and coffee, cleared down, washed up, taken stock and packed everything away ready for returning to stores at the end of the trip. Our day's work would usually be completed by around 9 pm, and some of us would go to the pub for a couple of beers before going home. We all knew that we had one day off before heading out to the Highlands for a weekend trip again.

Thursday was my only full day off most weeks during the summer season, from May to October. I would get up late, make sure all my work uniforms were ready for the weekend, pack my case for the upcoming trip, and head out to look around some record shops or just walk around London for an hour or two. I have always found London a fascinating city and I can still spend hours walking around there to this day. Thursday evening, I might pop down to the local pub in Upper Tulse Hill for a pint or two, or as often as not I didn't bother to go out at all. I might play the new records I had bought or watch television. I knew Friday would be a busy day!

We would report for work late morning on Fridays. We had between 60 and 70 passengers to look after on our weekend trips. We would leave from St Pancras station on Friday evening, and the whole afternoon would be spent preparing the train, making sure that everything looked immaculate. It was great to have a job where you had time to take pride in what you did. It did take a lot of time, but I remember standing on the platform at St. Pancras on those Friday evenings, greeting my customers, helping them with my bags, and knowing that I was part of an elite team. Not just any old railway steward could, or would have done this job. I was proud to be doing what I did.

Friday nights we would serve our passengers what could often turn into an elongated dinner, as they relaxed and unwound with a few drinks. It was often past 1 am when the last of them tottered off to their sleeping cars after perhaps one too many brandies or liqueurs, and we had to set up for breakfast before going to bed ourselves. Fortunately, the crew had proper sleeping berths on these weekend trips, so we were able to get a relatively good night's sleep, although often only for three or four hours, as we had breakfast service quite early.

Our passengers would emerge from their sleeping berths into the day cars by about 7.30, and we had to have tea and coffee available as soon as they sat down. Our washing and shaving was done in toilets again. This was not easy for me as I was used to bathing every morning, and didn't really feel right, but it was what everyone else did, so I got used to it. There was talk at one time about having a staff carriage with a shower built in, but that idea never came to fruition.

After breakfast had been served on the Saturday morning, our passengers would get off the train and go on a boat trip from Oban to the island of Iona. We would have to provide them with a packed lunch, which was delivered to the train already prepared, so we just had to distribute it. Once the passengers had sailed off to Iona, we had the rest of the day to prepare for serving dinner, relax, sleep, or go to the pub. We would usually prepare everything as quickly as we could and then go off and do our own thing. Chas and I would go for a walk and then have a few pints in a pub near Oban station. When we got back to the train, we would have a meal that the chef had prepared for us and then sleep for an hour, before being up, bright eyed and bushy tailed to greet our customers again. Saturday night usually meant Roast Beef and Yorkshire Pudding for the passengers, often with lashings of red wine. We would arrive in Fort William around 10 pm and the whole train, including all the staff, would decamp to a large hotel for the night.

'Time for a couple of pints' became a well-used sentence on these weekends. We were rarely, if ever, drunk (well, I wasn't) but it did sometimes feel as if we lived for the times when we could get off the train for a beer or two. So, after a couple of pints in the hotel bar, often bought for us by our appreciative customers, we would head off to bed. Breakfast was also in the hotel, and it was lovely to sit down and be waited on ourselves, for a change.

Our customers would be going down to Mallaig on a steam train shortly after breakfast. Half of our crew would go with them to serve tea and coffee on the way, and to collect and distribute a delicious fish and chip lunch for them when they arrived at the picturesque town at the end of the West Highland line. If it wasn't my turn to go on the trip to Mallaig, I would make my way to the train by around 11 am, and have a serious tidy-up of the kitchen vehicle before starting on the preparations for that evening's dinner service. I would be joined by other members of the team as and when they decided to turn up, but I was usually the first one there. Once the work had been done, I liked to sit down with a Sunday paper and relax. Sometimes I would go to the pub with some of the others at lunchtime, sometimes I wouldn't.

Those of us who weren't on the Mallaig trip always had a delicious lunch cooked by our chef, Bert. Sometimes, when he was in a good mood, which wasn't very often, he would make a fresh steak pie with vegetables and gravy for us.

Sunday evening dinner was always a special occasion on the Highlander trips. It was the passengers' last night with us – they had fillet steak for their main course and we always had to serve while travelling on the West Coast Main Line toward London. We also had to settle up with them for the drinks they had bought over the weekend – some had bills that ran into hundreds of pounds and we had to keep a very strict tally of what everyone had bought. This was also the time that they would give us our tips – it wasn't at all unusual to get between £50 and £80 from a couple. This was in the late 1980's. We were often receiving between £60 and £80 each in tips from one of these trips, which was on top of our wages. It was worth the hard work and lack of sleep!

So, after serving breakfast on Monday morning we would clear up, pack up, and that would be the end of another week, and the start of a new one.

The drinking on duty would not happen now. I never actually drank on a train, but there were those who did. In 1992, the entire railway industry became subject to a Drugs and Alcohol Policy. People would now be sacked for drinking on duty, or for reporting for work under the influence of alcohol or illegal drugs.

Chapter 9

People Get Married

Some of my friends had started getting married. John and Cathy were the first. They had been living together in London for some time and got married, they said, to keep Cathy's family happy. Cathy's Dad was a lovely man, a Chief Superintendent in the police, and I had been to the family home in Southend several times. I didn't tell him about my chequered past, otherwise he might have changed his opinion of me.

I was very surprised and totally delighted to be asked to be John's best man. As I mentioned before, he had been adopted, and didn't know his birth family at that point, so we had a certain affinity in that we had been separated from our families by events in our lives. I bought a new suit, shirt and tie for the wedding and had my hair, what was left of it, cut.

The wedding was held in a register office in North London, so thankfully there was no need for me to visit a church, which would still have been difficult for me, even after ten years away from religion. There was only the bride and groom, close family from both sides, and myself. Cathy's father took everyone for lunch at a very good Italian restaurant afterwards and then some friends of John and Cathy's threw a party for them at a big shared house. I remember thinking that if I ever got married I would like to have an informal wedding like that. John and I sat in the garden during the evening and shared a bottle of vodka, which I think was a rather an unusual thing for a bridegroom and his best man to do, but it seemed like a good idea at the time.

For many years John and I thought of each other as best friends. I remember promising him, not long after he and Cathy were married, to look after her if anything ever happened to him.

Not too long after they were married, John and Cathy gave up their flat in Muswell Hill and moved back to the Southend area, buying a flat in Leigh-on-Sea. I would sometimes go down and spend some of my rare free weekends with them, always partaking of a very liquid lunch on the Sunday at Cathy's parents' home. We would often watch 'The Big Match' on television after lunch, and this was where I first came into contact with 'broadsheet' Sunday newspapers, such as the Sunday Times and The Observer. I was a confirmed Daily Mirror reader myself, at the time, as a Labour voter, but my friendships were starting to bring me into contact with people from many different backgrounds. Again, these were occasions where I felt happy and accepted by 'normal' people.

I have to confess that from the mid-1980's onwards work more-or-less always came first in my life. After a year or so on the charter trains, the Chief Steward I was working with, Eric, had a breakdown and didn't appear at work for some weeks. Fortunately, all the staff were very experienced and we managed to carry on without him, but the show couldn't go on without a leader forever. Chas and I were looking after the paperwork and ordering together, with me doing most of the writing, but it was obvious that we needed a replacement for Eric if he wasn't coming back to work.

I was working on the charter trains at the time of the dreadful King's Cross fire in 1987. That particular day I had been working on a normal main line service; we had been delayed arriving back into King's Cross from Scotland because of 'a fire'. We had not been given any details. Eventually, our train pulled on to a platform at Finsbury Park station, just a few minutes from King's Cross, and terminated there. I decided to jump off there and catch the Victoria Line home to Brixton. No pub for me that night.

The Victoria Line train that I was on actually went through King's Cross station at a reduced speed at the height of the fire. I had no idea of the severity of the situation until I arrived home and put on the television news. If the train I was working had been due into King's Cross an hour earlier, I could well have been travelling down that same escalator at the time the fire started. I felt very fortunate, but devastated for the people who lost their lives. I spent the evening wondering if any of my friends and colleagues from work had been caught up in the fire, and feeling very fortunate that I had not been affected myself. In those days, smoking was permitted everywhere on the London Underground – I had smoked many a cigarette there myself, as well as on the top deck of London buses.

I had recently made a new friend, Jaz, who had come on to the charter train crews from Scotland. We both enjoyed a drink, and were younger than some of the old salts on the crew, so we tended to spend quite a bit of time together and had started meeting up occasionally outside of work.

It was approaching Christmas and New Year and I had not had a holiday for months. There was plenty of money in the bank as I was making virtually twice as much money working on the charter trains as I had made before, but never had the chance to spend it. Jaz and I decided to go off to Tenerife for a fortnight to celebrate the New Year. I began to look forward to it very much after a punishing routine of charter train rosters.

We had a lot of special trains running in the weeks immediately before Christmas, and hardly had any time off. I was at home one day, an increasingly rare event, when the phone rang. It was Trevor, our boss. He asked me if I would be interested in taking on the Chief Steward's role on the charter trains on a permanent basis.

I was very excited but also nervous. How would the rest of the crew take it? Here I was, the youngest, and arguably the most inexperienced member of the team, potentially taking charge of the crew. I explained to Trevor that I was going on a fortnight's holiday over the New Year period and that I would give him an answer when I returned.

The next day we were loading up a train and I spoke to all the team individually. I asked each of them how they would feel if I took over the position of Chief Steward and whether they would support me if I agreed to take on the role. I felt I could not just step into the role without finding out how they each felt.

Each of them said that they appreciated the fact that I had consulted them, that they were not interested in the position themselves, and that I should go for it with their support. Chas also said that he would support me, and as the rest of the team respected him, that helped me to make my decision. In those days, there was a very strict procedure that should have been followed when a promotion became available, but my boss had decided to sidestep the procedure. He said he wanted someone reliable who knew how everything worked and was happy to get their hands dirty. The railway was still heavily unionised, despite the closed shop having been made illegal by that time, and there were a few mutterings from one of the union representatives at King's Cross but no-one really stood in my way.

I went away on my holiday to Tenerife with Jaz, with my mind almost made up. I had thought that I would talk it over with Jaz while we were away, but that didn't really happen. Jaz turned out to be one of those people who, when on holiday, drank from about 11 am until 4 am the next day and then slept, either in bed or on a sunbed outside, for the rest of the time. He had not warned me about this aspect of his character. It wasn't to be a conversational holiday. After a few days, Jaz decided to get off with a girl who was staying in the next door apartment.

He certainly made me look like a complete amateur in the drinking department!

I was left to try to entertain myself, and thought I would entertain the said young lady's friend, but she made it very obvious that she was not remotely interested in me, so I spent a lot of the two weeks on my own. I remember one night we had gone out as a foursome to one of the bars in Veronicas, in Playa de las Americas, and after an hour this delightful young woman asked me to walk her home as she was bored!

In my times alone, I dwelt on the offer Trevor had made me, wondering if I could step up and on to the next level in my work. I had looked forward to discussing the ins and outs with Jaz, but that was obviously not going to happen. Not for the first time in my life, I realised that I had to make a decision alone, and after taking a couple of long walks, I decided to take up the challenge of the promotion that I had been offered.

And so it came to pass that I took on a leadership role for the first time in my life. The team I was leading were all my former colleagues. Most, if not all of them were more experienced than I. Barry and Tom had recently retired, and I had been given two very experienced stewards who had come from the Orient Express. Oliver was a lovely man in his fifties who worked as hard as any thirty-year old that I have ever met and never missed a day's work or an opportunity to have a laugh. He was gay, and had been in a relationship with his long-term partner for many years. Oliver was one of my favourite work colleagues of all my time on the railway, because he always had a positive attitude and a kind word for everyone. Quentin had also come from the Orient Express and was very professional and good with the customers, although I always felt that it was a bit of an act. I think he resented being managed by someone younger and less experienced than him. Chas stayed with me, and fortunately Lenny The Poser had decided to go back to the main line services as he was newly-married and his new wife was keen to have him at home more often. I can't say that I was sorry to see him go! Robert was another steward on the team who would always do just enough work but never really pushed himself. He knew just exactly how much he could get away with and wasn't really part of the team. Robert had to be told exactly what was expected of him before every meal service; as long as I remembered to do that things usually went smoothly. If I ever asked him why he had not completed a task he would tell me that I hadn't specifically told him to do it. It wasn't that he was unable to think for himself, the problem was that he thought he wasn't paid to think. The crew was completed by Bert the chef and his constantly-changing team of assistants. I remember one lad, George, from Derby who worked in the kitchen with us. One day we were all sitting down having a break on a Scottish weekend trip when I asked Bert where George was.

'He's making mayonnaise for tomorrow,' he said.

I asked Bert why George was making mayonnaise from scratch when I knew for certain that the other chefs ordered their mayonnaise ready-made. Trying to make mayonnaise on a moving train was quite a challenge, I would imagine. Bert replied that he was trying to make him into a proper chef, at which there were howls of laughter from the team. Everyone knew that Bert would never have got a job as a chef anywhere else, but he was reliable and there were rarely any complaints about his food, so we learned to live with his foibles. Another of Bert's assistants was Norman from Norwich, who for some reason was christened Mrs. Bridges. That could have been because he had a penchant for making cakes. I remember him being the first, and only, person, that I saw put both sugar and salt into carrots when he was cooking them – he said it brought out the flavour better, and who was I to disagree?

I decided to put into practice some of the ideas I had learned from Jack a year or two earlier. As I was the youngest member of the team by about ten years, I had more energy and that meant that I could work as part of the team during service and then do my paperwork when the others were taking a break. I was determined not to set myself above the rest of the team – I saw my role as facilitating great service and making quite a difficult job as easy as possible. I always tried to listen to the team and it paid dividends because they would do almost anything for me.

Serving 120 full silver service meals on a train moving at over 100 miles per hour is something that requires skill, precision, teamwork and a sense of humour, especially when you are working with thirty-year old equipment, as we were. The main attraction of working on the charter trains for me was the freedom. Our boss pretty much let us get on with it, and I have never been too great at being told what to do by someone who has never done my job. Obviously the pay was also better than working on the main line trains, because we were rarely at home, so we earned a lot of money and had little time off to spend it.

Being in charge of the kitchen team was probably the most challenging part of the job. Generally, in the catering business, the head waiter (which is effectively what I was) would not have any responsibility for the kitchen staff. I can't imagine what it might have been like to try and manage some of the chefs that I had seen in large London hotels a few years earlier. Everyone was terrified of them. Bert was an elderly Irish cook who had a great fondness for the drink and smoked strong untipped cigarettes constantly. I had known him since I had started on the railway, and had become adept at gauging when was a good time to talk to him and when to leave him alone. I remember very early one morning asking him for a cigarette, as I had run out, and nearly passing out after taking one drag. I'm sure his lungs must have been made of steel.

Bert had a wife and six children, three of whom worked on the railway at the time. He was part of the furniture on the railway, no-one could remember when he had started work there, and he wasn't a talkative man, so I never asked him about his career. His attitude, especially when he had had a drink, was very much that the kitchen was the most important piece in the jigsaw, because, without him, the 'outside' staff, as he called us, couldn't do our jobs. Of course, he was right, but I was keen to promote the idea of all being part of one team, and no-one being more important than anyone else. He did eventually develop a grudging respect for me, which was mutual.

As we had two kitchens on the train most of the time, we were usually teamed up with Ron and his crew at the other end of the train from us. Ron was a former main line Chief Steward from Euston, on the West Coast Main Line, so there was some friendly rivalry between us, as most of our team had been based at King's Cross at some time in their career on the railway. Think Arsenal and Tottenham – the railway equivalent was Euston and King's Cross! We would compete on the level of service we thought we delivered, who sold the most wine at dinner, and who got the most tips, too, if I'm honest. Ron's chef, Michael, had the edge on Bert, if I was honest, and he was a happy-go-lucky West Indian guy who I got on very well with. Ron had a couple of female members of staff on his crew who were rather attractive, so I used to find excuses to walk through the train to see them from time to time. They were both in relationships, so nothing happened for me there!

I must have been incredibly fit in those days because, although I still drank quite heavily and smoked like a chimney, I ate reasonably well and spent at least three or four days a week running up and down trains.

I realised during the first few weeks that I was in charge of this team that I was going to have to change my ways and try to be a role model for people who were older and more experienced than myself if I was going to make a success of this new job. We were quite a heavy drinking crew, and would find a way to get to the pub at every possible opportunity.

One Saturday at Oban I decided that I wasn't going to go to the pub. I caught up with all my paperwork, which included placing written food orders for the special trains we were working for the next few weeks and made myself a pot of tea. I sat and looked out of the window across the sea and wondered if I really needed to drink quite as much as I had been doing for so long. There had to be more to life!

A few weeks later, on the same West Highland trip, I had good cause to be thankful for that decision. Chas and Quentin, who had struck up what I thought was a most unlikely friendship came back on the train just before it was due to leave Oban in a high state of intoxication. I was frankly amazed, because I knew Chas well and had been very surprised when he hadn't turned up back on the train in time to do the preparation work that was needed before we served dinner. The rest of the crew had had to rally round and do Chas and Quentin's prep work and hadn't been impressed. I felt that they were testing me. I made no comment apart from to ask them if they were fit to work. They weren't really, but I had no option but to let them work, otherwise the customers would not have been served.

We arrived in Fort William that evening and after we had finished tidying up we all walked across to the hotel where we were staying for the night. Chas and I walked up to the room that we always shared.

'You alright mate?' he asked, when we got to our room.

'Not really Chas, no,' I replied. 'I was disappointed in you today, to be honest, coming back to the train in that state.'

He didn't reply, and we went down to the bar for a drink. No more was said, but it got back to me a few days later that he had let the rest of the crew know that I had 'pulled him up' about his behaviour, and there was never any repeat of that incident. This was a man who was old enough to be my father, married with three sons and a reputation as a man who spoke his mind and wasn't afraid to back it up.

A few years later, when I got married, Chas and his wife were among the people who had to be 'pruned' from my wedding invitation list, because we were limited to 80 people at the venue. I understand that he was not impressed not to have been invited, and I never saw or heard from him again after that. I had left the charter train crew by the time I was married, and having to omit Chas from the wedding meant the end of our friendship. He was a great colleague and a brilliant support to me when we worked together.

Chapter 10

More Changes and I Turn Thirty

I had a brief dalliance with my friend John's younger sister during the time I was working on the charter trains. John and Cathy had their first child, a daughter, Rachel, and asked me to be godfather to her. I was very flattered but tried my best to get out of it as I had never attended any sort of church service up to this point, since leaving home in 1973. However, John persisted, and I found myself attending a high Anglican church mass at which Rachel was christened. I had treated myself to a new suit for the occasion, a Prince of Wales check double-breasted number, and did look rather smart, if I say so myself. I noticed Iain's sister, also named Cathy, eyeing me up during the course of the day, and asked her for her phone number. I rang her later that week and she sounded very keen. I was flattered because she was only 19 and very pretty. I had met her once or twice before but thought she was too young for me. Well, she probably was, but we had a very enjoyable fling for a few weeks and it did wonders for my self-confidence. I remember inviting her round to my flat for dinner and cooking salmon, something that we regularly served on the trains. I had learned to cook poached salmon from our chefs at work. The meal went down very well and we had a great evening together.

One Sunday I invited Cathy to come out on a train that I was working from Marylebone to Stratford-upon-Avon. It was a regular trip that we did, serving a roast lunch to our passengers on the way to Stratford and afternoon tea on the return trip. We had a steam engine on and had to work very hard to get everything done in time for our passengers to get off at Stratford and stretch their legs for an hour while we prepared to serve afternoon tea. Cathy sat in one of the passenger coaches and enjoyed a complimentary roast beef lunch and a couple of glasses of wine. She was much younger than the other passengers and I think she felt a bit out of place. When we arrived at Stratford the crew insisted that I got off the train with Cathy and took her for a walk. I was very touched as it was probably the one time that they needed me to stay and work with them to get the train prepared, but they all insisted that I spent some time with Cathy.

After that I was quite pushy and tried to make something long-term out of the relationship with Cathy, but it soon became clear that she was not as enthusiastic as I was, and there was an eleven-year age difference, so we parted company and I have never seen Cathy again to this day.

I turned thirty in 1986. I decided that I wanted to do something quite different for my birthday and spend it with my 'middle class' friends. About ten of us spent the evening in The Fridge, a trendy nightclub of the time, in Brixton. I remember it was all painted in black, inside and out, and there were old domestic appliances such as fridges and washing machines dotted about ornamentally inside the club, which was a converted cinema. The music system was ear-splittingly loud, but the music was fantastic and I remember thinking I was very cool in my tweed coat, trousers with braces to hold them up, collarless shirt and brogues. I think we all felt a little bit out of our depth as none of us made a habit of going night clubbing – perhaps I was growing up now that I was 30! It would have been around the same time that I went to The Fridge to see a band called 'Curiosity Killed The Cat' who were popular for a short time, and I also remember visiting the Camden Palace in North London with Nick, Karen and some friends of theirs who lived the other side of the river.

The visit to Camden Palace was memorable because I took some so-called magic mushrooms that night, the one and only time in my life that I ever indulged in any drugs apart from alcohol and cannabis – magic mushrooms were definitely not for me. Suffice to say that I remember nothing about the evening apart from a lot of noise and flashing lights.

Chapter 11

More 80s

My good friends Nick and Karen were married in the late 1980s. Nick was from a small town in Wales, and Karen came from a very middle-class background west of London, and in some ways they were like chalk and cheese, but they obviously loved each other very much.

When they first met, Karen had already planned to go away travelling for the best part of a year, and it says something about their relationship that she did go away, with his blessing. He tried very hard to pretend he didn't miss her while she was away, but I don't think many people were fooled. I remember how delighted they were to be back together when Karen returned from her travels.

They had their stag and hen nights on the same evening, and both parties ended up in the same pub, the *Duke of Devonshire* in Balham High Road. They were inseparable, and have remained so until the time of writing this.

Nick asked me to be an usher at the wedding, which was held near Karen's mother's lovely home in Middlesex. I was still very uneasy about going to churches at this time but was very proud to be asked to be an usher. I spent a lot of the day organising people as there were several different elements to the celebrations. I was thrilled to be asked and felt great about the whole experience.

The reception was held at Karen's mother's house. The weather was very kind and the champagne and wine flowed all day. Nick and Karen had booked a function room at a local pub for the evening do so that their friends could let their hair down a bit. Karen's very lovely grandmother was related to a Lord, so we had to be on our best behaviour at the house. Nearly everyone smoked in those days but most people thought their parents didn't know they smoked, so that was another reason for being away from our elders for the evening party. Nick and Karen's first dance was to Nina Simone's *My Baby Just Cares For Me*, which had been re-released a year or so earlier and was perfect for them.

It was a brilliant day and when, at the end of the day I was herding everyone into a minibus for the journey back to South London, Nick told me that he wished he had asked me to be his best man, as I had done more to make the day a success than the actual best man had. That meant a lot to me as I still didn't have a great amount of self-esteem, even though I had a reasonably successful life by this time. To be accepted by normal people still meant a lot to me.

Nick and Karen had bought a cottage in North Norfolk as their marital home, but they were not able to move into it immediately after the wedding. They were looking for a place to rent short-term, and I offered them my sofa bed and front room for a few weeks. So, I had lodgers, for the first and only time in my life. I was away a lot with work, but I did find it difficult sharing my abode with other people, after several years of living alone. One night I arrived home from work at 4am, very tired, to find that my friends and flat mates had held a dinner party for some of their friends, and had not only left the washing up, but had drunk a bottle of good wine that I had been saving for a special occasion! Much as I liked both Nick and Karen, I was glad to have my small flat to myself again when their cottage was ready.

Eventually they moved into their dream cottage in the North Norfolk countryside and I went down in the van with them to help them move in. I remember the journey from South London to Norfolk well, and the part of the country that they moved to has had a special place in my heart since those days. I remember helping them unpack and realising that this was the end of an era – no longer would I have my great friends Nick and Karen so close to me. There were very mixed feelings as I was glad to have my flat back to myself again!

A few months later they had a combined New Year's and house warming party, and a number of us from London went down for a wonderful long weekend in the country. I remember us all going to their friendly and welcoming local country pub for dinner on New Year's Eve and how great I felt, being part of this wide circle of friends, all of whom had had a normal upbringing, were well-educated and great fun to be with. I felt extremely lucky. It meant a lot to me, after my unusual upbringing, to find a group of people who accepted me for who I was and welcomed me into their circle. I had felt like an outsider for most of my life up until the mid 1980s, possibly right up until that moment.

Nick and Karen both found teaching jobs in Norfolk, and I became a regular visitor at their cottage in a small village in North Norfolk, near the country town of Holt. Nick and I saw eye-to-eye on many topics, including politics and sometimes music. I noticed that Nick got into classical music after he moved out of London. He explained this by saying that he was so far away from the centre of culture in London now that he had decided to get into some music that didn't change so often, so that he was more able to keep up with it. I have several classical CD's that I bought around that time and I enjoy relaxing and listening to classical music on a Sunday evening sometimes, while preparing myself for the week ahead.

I was in my early thirties with a good job, albeit one that took me away from home a great deal, had a varied circle of friends, my own home, the money to do pretty much what I wanted to do and I felt that I belonged, both at work, where I was respected, and in my various friendships. Sometimes I would have days where I felt completely bereft of self-esteem and would not leave the flat, but mostly I kept busy and managed to stave off the depression that wanted to take over.

I was already an avid cricket fan, but my joy in this wonderful game deepened and I would attend games at The Oval and Lord's regularly, often alone, as I loved to watch the game uninterrupted. I watched the great West Indies and Australian teams of the time and found an affinity with cricket-loving people that remains with me to this day. It is possible to get into conversation with a complete stranger at a cricket match and discuss a mutual love of the game and the people who surround it. I also became a fan of Test Match Special, the BBC cricket commentary radio show in the 1980s, when the great John Arlott and Brian Johnston were commentating. I would often watch Test match cricket on the television at home while listening to the radio commentary, which was so much better-informed and entertaining than the television commentary in those days, and still is.

I still enjoyed live music and went to see bands such as Kid Creole and The Coconuts, The Neville Brothers, Tom Waits and once, memorably, Elvis Costello and The Attractions. Costello and the band were on stage at the Hammersmith Palais for three-and-a-half hours, probably the best live gig I ever went to in my life, although it is difficult to compare the feelings from different music.

It would have been around this time that I started to get interested in walking as a hobby. My friend Mel introduced me to the joys of walking – he would hitch-hike down to Cornwall and I would take the train, as I could travel free with my railway passes, and we would stay in bed and breakfasts and walk the Cornish coastal path every day for a week to ten days. There is nothing in the world like the English countryside, in my opinion, and I still spend many enjoyable hours walking in all weathers. There is no such thing as bad weather, only ill-preparation and poor equipment. I remember one memorable trip to Cornwall where we had booked into a bed and breakfast on Lizard Point and gone for a walk around to see what was on offer for lunch. We pitched up at a small hotel where there was a hog roast going on in preparation for a party that evening. We were asked if we would like to help roast the hog, which involved turning a whole pig on a spit over an open fire for an hour or two, in exchange for a free beer or two. Well, it would have been churlish to refuse, so we started drinking at about 3 pm and wandered back to our bed and breakfast much later that evening, bellies full of Cornish ale and fresh roast pork.

The Tooting crowd that I had been friendly with for several years all seemed to split up and go in different directions at the same time. Some got married, some went and worked abroad. Tom and Jo, my friends from Crystal Palace separated, and Nick and Karen had moved away. I consoled myself with the idea that I had friends in Norfolk whom I could visit, and I spent several lovely weekends there, often with Tamsin, as she was also Karen's best friend. Tamsin was probably the first single woman that I was friends with where there was no romantic interest from either of us. We enjoyed a lot of the same music and activities, and genuinely enjoyed each other's company without there being any attraction between us.

Work continued to be very busy and time consuming, especially in the summer. We would work a Scottish land cruise train every weekend, departing on a Friday night and arriving back in London on a Sunday night or Monday morning. These were enjoyable because we were really able to build a relationship with the customers over the course of the weekend, but tiring because we had to work fifteen-hour days and were sleeping in railway sleeping cars two nights a week. We had a lot of returning customers and that often made it very special . I remember there was a lady who liked burnt toast with her breakfast, and the lovely couple who had a fruiterer's business and liked Muscadet. They were great people and always gave us a handsome tip.

On Wednesdays we would usually have a one-day trip from London to Leeds and then up the Settle and Carlisle line steam-hauled before returning down the West Coast main line into Euston. This involved loading and preparing the train on Tuesday afternoon and then working a very long, arduous day on the Wednesday. We had Thursday off, when I would spend half the day washing and ironing uniforms for the weekend trip. I was earning an absolute fortune by the standards of those days, with very little opportunity to spend the money.

One of Bert's kitchen assistants was Jonny, a decent sort of guy from Swindon. Bert had a lot of kitchen assistants because he gave them a hard time, working them as hard as he could, and they usually went back to the main line trains after a few months of doing his donkey work for him. One day Jonny let it be known in conversation that he had booked himself a three-week holiday in the Caribbean. I didn't know him all that well, but thought the idea of a holiday in the Caribbean sounded great. I had all that money burning a hole in my bank account and I needed a goal to get me through another summer of hard work.

I spoke to Jonny over a pint at the end of that trip and asked him if he fancied some company on the trip. He agreed, and said he would add me to the booking. I remember it was with Pegasus Holidays and it cost £1,500 for three weeks all-inclusive. I remember baulking slightly at the cost, but I felt that I had the money and deserved the holiday. I had never, even in my wildest dreams, believed that I would ever go to the Caribbean on holiday!

I would think very carefully before spending that much on a holiday now, so that puts into perspective the amount of money I was earning in the late 1980s.

Chapter 12

The Caribbean

I was tremendously excited about this holiday and probably bored everyone I knew for months before by going on about it. I had never been away for three weeks before and had to ask for special dispensation from work, as the railway had a rule that no-one was supposed to take more than two consecutive weeks off. We were to go away in November, which was outside the peak holiday period for railway staff, so the annual leave was granted.

I decided that I needed a whole new summer wardrobe if I was going to dress to impress in the Caribbean, but there was one problem. Burton's, my usual outfitters, did not sell summer clothes in the winter, so I took a trip to Oxford Street and went to Selfridge's. I spent a small fortune on Fred Perry leisure wear and went home and packed a large suitcase and a hold-all. It all added to my sense of excitement and the build up to the holiday of a lifetime.

You would have thought I was going on a six-month world cruise, but I wanted to be prepared for all eventualities.

I had to acquire my first full passport, as a British Visitors Passport was not valid in the Caribbean, and I was very excited when the day of the holiday arrived in November 1989. We were flying to St. Lucia on a British Airways scheduled service as there were no charter flights to the Caribbean at that time. We were on a 747 and there was free food and drink all the way. I indulged in quite a few large Bloody Mary's, something I had quite recently discovered, and was reasonably well-refreshed by the time we arrived in St. Lucia.

We were to stay in St. Lucia for one night before flying to the island of Canouan, one of the Grenadine Islands, adjacent to Mustique, where many famous people have holiday homes. On our arrival at the Halcyon Beach Club it was clear that we were in something of a minority, as we were the only pair of single guys on the holiday. There were also no obvious single women around, which was something of a concern, but I was so overwhelmed with the beauty of the place and the standards of the food and service that nothing else really mattered.

We had a great dinner in a semi-open air restaurant overlooking the sea and I'm sure we had a few glasses of liquid refreshment too. It would have been a shame not to; after all we had paid a small fortune for an all-inclusive holiday. This was my reward, I thought, as I sat back and surveyed the scene around me, for all those hours, days and weeks of running up and down trains looking after other people. Now it was my turn to be looked after!

The next morning we had an early start and we were taken out to a small airfield where we were to catch our flight to Canouan. That was where the adventure really started as we were put on board a small sixteen-seater propeller plane for the short journey to Canouan. It was by far the smallest plane I had been on and I was thrilled and terrified in equal measures. The scenery during the trip was breathtaking, when I could bring myself to look out of the aircraft window. We were flying over a number of small islands in the beautiful Caribbean Sea. It was like another world compared to the holidays I had experienced in Europe, and was an extraordinary experience from beginning to end.

Soon, we landed on the tiny airstrip on the minute island of Canouan. The immigration and passport control was situated in a small nissen hut and when the customs and immigration officer had checked our passports he poured us a plastic cup full of rum punch and welcomed us to the island. A far cry indeed from the welcome you receive when you enter most countries!

Outside the immigration hut there was a large old Bedford army truck. We were somewhat taken aback to be realise that this was to be our transport to the resort, a mile or so away. Six of us arrived together; we all piled on to the back of the army truck with our luggage and wondered where we were being taken as we bumped along the unmade road in the scorching heat. I remember questioning, silently, what we had let ourselves in for. I had not even seen the holiday brochure and had no real idea what to expect. I thought I had better not say anything to anybody about just how little I knew about this holiday I had booked! When we arrived at the Canouan resort it was fabulous. Not five-star luxury, just incredibly welcoming and friendly staff, lovely villas on the beach to stay in, and sand so soft that your feet sank into it. I had never seen anywhere so beautiful in my life.

Jonny and I were quite obviously the only male twosome on the island, but I decided I was going to make the most of the holiday, and to be honest, the whole place was just so awesome I could have enjoyed it on my own. There was a bar on the beach, and the restaurant was also semi *al fresco* so the only time we had to be indoors was at night.

We had arrived in time for lunch, which was a selection of barbecued chicken and fish with delicious fresh salad. Plain, but fresh and wonderful food, and that set the pattern for the rest of the holiday. I thought that I had earned a rest, and it was certainly what I had for those two weeks on Canouan.

The bar served rum punch from just after breakfast, and other drinks were available too. We had nothing to pay for, absolutely nothing; apart, that is, from the insect repellent. We were told that we would need to cover ourselves from head to foot in insect repellent in the evenings, even if we were wearing trousers and long-sleeved shirts. Mosquitoes apparently had a habit of making life very unpleasant for white people who weren't wearing repellent, so Jonny and I bought large aerosol sprays of rather nasty insect repellent and sprayed ourselves liberally with it every time we came out of a shower. It cost about £6 a can, and I got through four cans in a fortnight. There was very little else to spend money on as all the food and drink was included.

I could have stayed on Canouan for the rest of my life, but if I had there is a good chance that I would have finished up an alcoholic. The first night I was there, Jonny and I were sitting at the bar chatting to some of the other guests when I noticed a huge display of large cans of Libby's tomato juice behind the bar. I asked the attractive and very friendly young local barmaid what she did with the tomato juice.

'Nothing really,' she replied, ' we just have it there.'

I asked her if she knew how to make a Bloody Mary, and she shook her head shyly.

'Would you like me to show you?' I asked.

'OK,' she said, and motioned me to come behind the bar with her.

I managed to find all the ingredients for the perfect Bloody Mary – vodka, tomato juice, ice, lime and lemon juice, Worcestershire and Tabasco sauces, and a jug. I made a large jug of Bloody Mary, placed it on the bar and then poured myself a glass. It was delicious, and I asked the other guests if they would like to try some. They all turned up their noses, so I was left to drink it all myself.

Now, Bloody Mary is one of those drinks that you can drink a lot of – at least I can. You don't really notice anything until you try to stand up, and then you find that you haven't got any legs. Well, I found myself legless on numerous occasions during that holiday, but it didn't matter. It was that sort of holiday – totally relaxed.

The resort had a catamaran that held about twenty people, and it would go out to a different neighbouring island every day. Jonny and I decided that we would take a trip out on the catamaran every other day, and stay and enjoy the delights of Canouan on the other days. I couldn't walk past the bar without having a jug of Bloody Mary put in front of me, and the staff were personally slighted if anyone ever decided to miss a meal. The catamaran carried beer and wine, and the crew would barbecue lunch wherever they dropped anchor at the appropriate time of day. We would take turns in holding on to the fishing line out the back of the boat on our way back to Canouan in the afternoon, and one memorable day I found myself helping to land a large red snapper, which we had for dinner that evening. Marvellous!

I also discovered lobster on that holiday. It was something I had never really experimented with before, and I was a bit dubious to start with, but I tried it one night and was hooked. In the Caribbean no-one will buy or eat a lobster that isn't fresh, so they are caught and then kept in wooden boxes underwater until they are going to be cooked. Then they are barbecued. Cruel and inhumane to the lobsters, I agree, but the taste is exquisite.

I became used to lobster and champagne for dinner. The resort was French-owned, and the British guests noticed that the French guests had champagne with dinner every night, whereas we only had it once a week. Someone had it out with the resort manager, and we suddenly started getting champagne every night too.

There were some great people on that holiday – sadly, as so often happens, I never met any of them again. There was an elderly couple there that I thought I recognised, and it turned out that they used to manage a pub near Grafton's in Westminster that I had used several years previously.

We met a lovely young couple from Ipswich, Tom and Jenny. They had been to the Caribbean together a few years previously and enjoyed it so much that they had both taken on second jobs so that they could afford a three-week holiday there every year. One day Jonny and I got together with them and hired one of the local fishing boats for the day to take us to Mustique, the neighbouring island. Philip, the fisherman, who also helped to crew the resort's catamaran sometimes, took us. The sea was usually very rough between the two islands and it was important to sail there and back at very specific times or the waters were impassable.

We left Canouan early in the morning, just after breakfast, and arrived in Mustique mid-morning after a choppy crossing. From there we had a tour of Mustique in a hired Mini Moke Jeep, seeing Princess Margaret's, Mick Jagger's and David Bowie's houses before having a late lunch in Basil's Bar in the harbour. I virtually lived on fish for that whole two weeks; it was extraordinary how great the food was. Basil's Bar was where the great and the good hung out in Mustique; there were pictures on the wall of Princess Margaret with a number of celebrities. We were the only celebrities there that day, though!

The journey back to Canouan from Mustique was not a happy one for my friend Jonny. The sea was very rough and Jonny had rather an appetite for the alcohol, so unfortunately was rather poorly on the return trip. Our sailor friend, Philip, who had taken us on the expedition, was at pains to tell us that not many holidaymakers made that journey by boat. He explained to us that most of the people who visited Mustique while on holiday on Canouan came over by air because of the rough sea. I had eaten and drunk just as much as everyone else, but, fortunately, I have a strong stomach and I was perfectly well on the return sailing.

The two weeks on Canouan was the most relaxing holiday I had experienced in my life up to that point. It was certainly a just reward for the past few years of hard work, and I would never have imagined, sixteen years before, in 1973, when I left my family behind to embark on my new life that I would ever travel to somewhere so exotic. I have nothing but great memories of that holiday, the beauty of the location and the overwhelming friendliness of the people. These days Canouan island is a 5-star luxury resort, but I preferred it when it was more basic, local and friendly.

One particular memory stands out. Jonny and I had taken a walk into the interior of the island one afternoon and were just in time to see thirty or so happy children come tumbling out of school. The people on Canouan were comparatively poor, but who could be unhappy in such a beautiful place?

143

The day before we were due to leave Canouan we decided to fly to St. Vincent for the day. Both Jonny and I had brought quite an amount of spending money with us, just in case, and we had spent virtually nothing apart from £20 each on insect repellent! We booked a flight from Canouan to St. Vincent and had a taxi pick us up at St. Vincent airport and take us on a tour of the island. It was the only time in my life that I have had a man waiting for me at an airport bearing a placard with my name on it!

St. Vincent was another beautiful island and we had a great day there being shown around. I particularly remember visiting the botanical gardens, where we had our own guide, and tasting 'raw' vanilla.

Our sojourn on Canouan was at an end and we were to spend the final week of the holiday on a small boat with about twenty other people cruising around the Grenadine Islands. I had brought far too much clothing and had not worn any of my expensively-acquired new shirts and trousers that I had brought with me. Shorts and t-shirts had been very much the order of the day, even most evenings, and I packed my unworn Fred Perry polo shirts away in a holdall. To start our cruise we had first to fly back to St. Lucia from where we were to set sail.

Our bags were on the airstrip waiting to be loaded into the small plane that was to fly us back to St. Lucia when there was a sudden cloudburst. It stopped raining almost as soon as it started, but the damage had been done. My holdall, which was not waterproof, was flooded. The colours in all my new, unworn Fred Perry polo shirts ran, and they all went in the bin when I got home.

We flew back to St. Lucia and were taken to the harbour, where the boat that was to be our home for the next week was moored. It was quite an old, small boat that Jonny and I immediately nicknamed the *Old Tub*. If any of our fellow guests had been expecting something more luxurious, no-one said anything. That evening we set sail back to the Grenadine Islands, having dinner and drinks on board ship for the first time in my life. Jonny and I slept in bunk beds in a small shared cabin with a shower just along the corridor where the water came out just fast enough to shower. It didn't matter that the water was almost cold, as the days and nights in the Caribbean were very warm.

Even though we had already visited all the Grenadine Islands on the catamaran from Canouan, we thoroughly enjoyed sailing around them again. We visited Petit St. Vincent, Tobago Cays, Palm Island, and had an emotional reunion with our friends on Canouan, where I was once again persuaded to drink a jug of Bloody Mary. I went brown for the first time in my life as my fair skin was tanned by the combination of the hot sun and the sea breezes. The crew on the boat included a young Afro-Caribbean lady in her early twenties, and true to form, I fell a little bit in love with her. Unfortunately, she had a boyfriend ashore, and my feelings were not reciprocated.

It really was the most wonderful trip, plentiful fresh food, wonderful scenery, friendly and welcoming people and plenty of beer, wine and champagne.

I probably wouldn't have felt too comfortable on a 'proper' cruise ship – indeed we saw some massive American vessels as we cruised around the Grenadine islands, and once or twice almost got caught in their wash, but our little *Old Tub*, with its small cabins with bunk beds, a little reminiscent of railway sleeping cars, was just right for me.

Jonny and I got on well with the other 'inhabitants' of the boat, although we were the only single people aboard.

Eventually, the holiday of a lifetime drew to a close. We anchored back in St. Lucia and were to spend our final night in the Caribbean back in the Halcyon Beach Club, where we had started our holiday three weeks earlier. It had been, by some distance, the best holiday I had ever experienced. I had often heard people say that they hadn't wanted to go home from a particularly enjoyable holiday, but that was the first time that I had experienced that feeling.

On the last day we joined together with some of the people that we had got to know over the three weeks and decided to go out for lunch. None of us had spent very much money while we had been away, apart from on souvenir t-shirts, of which I had a large collection, having bought one from every island we had visited. There were a number of local restaurants advertised in the Halcyon Beach Club foyer, and, after some friendly discussion, we picked one that advertised ta collection and drop off service, to and from any hotel, for any diners. . We called to book, and a little later a rather ramshackle little minibus arrived and picked us all up. We arrived at the restaurant a few miles away, whereupon the driver of the minibus disappeared, re-appearing a few moments later to show us to our table and take our orders. He then went away, cooked and served a delicious lunch with wine, cleared the table, and for all I know washed up as well before he delivered us back to our hotel where we had to prepare for our imminent departure back to the UK.

Lasting memories of the Caribbean? Lovely, genuine, friendly people who, despite being relatively poor themselves, were extremely generous. Great food, fabulous Bloody Marys, soft almost white sand and crisps made from sliced bananas, which I have never been able to replicate at home.

I am thankful to the railway for many things, but my job on the railway provided the opportunity to have this wonderful Caribbean experience, and that holiday will live on in my mind forever.

We flew back to the UK on another British Airways 747 and had the most amazing service, including a visit to the flight deck. I had discovered how the other half lived, and I liked it!

Chapter 13

Back to Reality

Going back to work after that holiday was a bit of a struggle, because it was late November, and my first day back at work was a day cleaning train kitchen vehicles at the freezing cold sidings in North London. My friend and colleague, Chas, and I had secured the unenviable job of keeping all the charter train fleet kitchen vehicles clean and equipped. That was all very well during the summer, but not so great in the winter. However, we often found that if we worked really hard for three days a week, in the winter, when there weren't so many charter trains, we could often get away early on the other two days. It also meant that we were excused working the normal service trains in the winter when there was less demand for charter trains.

One of the big charter train jobs we did around that time was for the Methodist Church. It was the 200th anniversary of the birth or death of John Wesley and several hundred

American Methodists came over to the UK to tour around a number of places of interest in the history of their church. They had hired two trains for ten days.

There were endless meetings and telephone conversations about this job. Initially, the Methodists had stipulated that all the staff had to be practising Christians – that one brought a bit of a hollow laugh when we first heard it. The people that worked with me were, on the whole, very decent, hard-working folk, none of them were particularly religious, and we had to tell our Methodist friends that this particular rule was just about unenforceable. Then they stipulated that there was to be no alcohol on board either of the trains for the duration of the week. It was just as well that the one member of my team who couldn't do without a drink was a gin drinker, as that looked like water, especially as he took it with lemonade and no ice or lemon! It was, of course, still before 1992, when the railway introduced strict drugs and alcohol regulations. At the time I worked on the charter trains, there was no regulation for catering staff drinking on duty, and many took advantage of that situation.

In the end, the trip went quite smoothly. The Methodists were quite decent people. We ran around after them for ten days, although I had made sure that anyone in the team who wanted to have a night at home during the trip was able to. They were the only Americans that I had ever served in my entire life who did not leave a single penny in tips. I had also never seen people who drank so many soft drinks. Our trains were stacked to the rafters with cases of cola, lemonade and fizzy orange when we left London, and we had to replenish our stocks twice during the ten day trip. We were used to having to order extra supplies of wine, but we had never run out of soft drinks before!

Eventually, after three mostly enjoyable years on the charter trains, I felt that enough was enough. I needed to have a life again. I had had three years of being abused by drunks on horse racing specials, including Cheltenham races and The Grand National. I had not had a weekend off for three years, apart from when I was on leave. However, I had enjoyed the camaraderie, the lovely customers on the land cruises and even the steam train enthusiasts on the steam specials had managed to find a place in my heart, strange though they were!

The crunch came the day that Trevor, our manager, had summoned me to a meeting on the only day off I had had in two weeks. I felt unappreciated. I knew that I was doing a better job than some of the other three Chief Stewards on the charter trains at the time. I knew I had the best crew and I knew there was no more I could do.

I went to the meeting with my boss and left feeling very dissatisfied with life. I decided to go to King's Cross, as it was late afternoon, and see if there was anyone around that I could have a drink with and a moan to! I had kept in touch with my friends at King's Cross and had often done a day or two's work there – not for me the attitude of some of the charter train staff who thought they were better than everyone else!

I went to the Great Northern Hotel bar and ordered myself a pint. A Chief Steward, Eddie, was in there, and I went to have a chat with him.

'Surprised you want to talk to me,' he said. 'You charter people think you're better than us, don't you?'

Eddie thought he was the master of the wind-up, but he cut no ice with me.

'No, not me mate,' I said. 'I'm fed up with the charters anyway.'

I proceeded to tell Eddie how I felt. He told me that it might be my lucky day.

'There's a Chief Steward's job going on the 7.50, Frosty,' he said. 'Why don't you go for that?'

The 7.50 was the Yorkshire Pullman from King's Cross to Leeds. This train had two Chief Stewards as the crew split halfway through the day. The job that was on offer involved working with my old friend Don, who I had enjoyed working with so much a few years previously. I decided to strike while the iron was hot.

All anyone had to do to apply for a promotion or sideways move on the railway in those days was fill in a form and

154

put it in to the staff office. All promotions were allocated on seniority; it was only if there were two people with the same amount of seniority applying for the same job that suitability would come into play. It seems incredible now, but people were never interviewed for those positions. If someone applied for a post, a week or a fortnight later they would receive a letter telling them if they had been successful or not. This was how people got on and up the promotion ladder in the railway industry in the late 1980s.

I left the Great Northern Hotel bar and went straight over to the office at King's Cross to put in my application for the Chief Steward's job on the Yorkshire Pullman. Then I went home to figure out how I was going to tell my boss that I was moving back to King's Cross.

In the end I didn't have to. He had a call from one of the managers at King's Cross early the next morning to see when he would release me. He rang me. To his credit, he didn't try too hard to persuade me to stay. I had worked for Trevor for three years and had given my all. He wasn't a bad boss, for someone who had never done the job himself. He kept out of the way when he knew his people were

doing a good job, which was all you could ask of a
manager in those days, I guess.

I had to tell my team that I was leaving them – that was
hard. I told them that I was still young and that I needed to
have a life outside of work. I thanked them and said that I
would come back and work a few trains with them now
and then to keep my hand in. I still wanted to be one of the
men made of steel who worked on the trains made of
wood, but I had to have a life too. I did feel torn, the three
years on the charter trains had been great for me, and I
knew I was taking a step backwards, which was something
I had vowed to myself never to do. At the same time, I was
looking forward to being part of another great team. I knew
Don had put a great bunch of people together on his
Pullman crew and I was looking forward to working with
them and having more of a life outside of work.

My first day back at King's Cross was spent with one of the
new young female managers down at the depot looking at
the brand new Mark IV electric trains that were being
introduced on the East Coast main line a few months later.
It hit me that I had now worked on the railway for over ten

years – long enough to see two new generations of trains enter service.

The new trains looked fantastic; they were like new cars with plastic covers on the seats, immaculate stainless steel kitchens and automatic machines to make announcements.

'You will never have to make another announcement,' proclaimed Abigail, the young manager who had the job of showing a group of us around the train.

I noticed that there were no shelves or storage space anywhere in the kitchen.

'No, that's all changing,' said Abigail. 'Everything you need will be brought to the train before you leave and will be taken off again when you get back. You won't have to do any washing up, you will be able to concentrate on serving your customers.'

Alarm bells started ringing in my head. Just faint ones, but they were there. They had tried this a few years ago at Euston and it had been an unmitigated disaster. The private company they had brought in to supply all the food, drink and equipment had lost millions of pounds and ended up walking away from the contract.

I thought perhaps our senior managers had learned from that experience and were going to manage it differently this time around. We would not have to wait long to find out. I really wanted to be positive as I loved working on the railway and had become a respected and valued member of the railway family during the past ten years. I knew how to deliver great service and I had spent three years learning how to lead a team to do the same. Now I wanted to put some of that learning into practice on the main line trains.

When I came off the charter trains, I used to say to people that there was a huge difference between the customers, or passengers, on the charter trains and those on the main line 'service' trains. The charter train customers, by and large, were there because they wanted to be. Most of the main line passengers were there because they had to be. I thought that if we could find a way of getting our main line passengers to travel because they wanted to, we would be on to a winner. I was just a little bit ahead of my time. In those days, the railway was purely operational. Everything was about trains, and people didn't really come into the equation, whether they were staff or passengers.

I started back on the trains at King's Cross a day or so after my day out at the sidings looking at the trains of the future. Someone had thought that it would be a good idea for me to have a trip out on the Yorkshire Pullman before I took over the team that I was to share with my old friend Don. I had a trip out with the crew that worked the Pullman on the opposite shift and noticed how they all knew exactly what they were doing and that there were no 'passengers' on the crew. We always used to say that there were some trains where you could have a 'weak link' or a 'passenger' on the crew; the Pullman was certainly not one of those. Eighty to ninety cooked silver service breakfasts and a busy buffet car, together with full at-seat service in a very busy first class, meant that everyone had to work hard, and non-stop, for just under two hours, and then they had half-an-hour to clear everything up, re-lay all the tables and work the train back to London again. There was very little preparation time and if a crew lost any time at all they could be what we used to refer to as 'up the wall'!

159

I realised that I had come back to a challenge but consoled myself that I would be at home in my own bed every night from now on, and that was worth a lot to me. I might have taken a slight drop in money but I could live on less than I had been earning, and I had a good few pounds salted away for a rainy day by that time too!

By and large, I really enjoyed being back at King's Cross. It allowed me to have a life again, and it was great to be working with Don . We were both committed to doing the job professionally and to having a good laugh at the same time. We were also fortunate to have a superb chef and a crew who could get over almost any challenge. We had a great Irish girl on the team who could virtually run the restaurant on her own, if necessary, and she enjoyed the challenge and always had a smile on her face.

Railway catering had a really bad name for many years, but there were always a number of us who took a pride in our work, tried to look after our customers and enjoy our work.

My social life outside of work was in some sort decline at this point. I had left the charter trains to try to have more of a life outside of work, but that had coincided with a number of my friends getting married and moving away, so I was faced with the prospect of making some new friends. Even Mel, my great friend of a number of years, had almost settled down with a charming girl, much younger than him, whom he had met on a walking holiday in Cornwall.

I had got myself into a bit of a rut, so I started staying in the pub after work for longer than I should have done, and working overtime when I didn't really want to. I would never have admitted it out loud to anyone, and often did not allow myself to admit it internally, but I was lonely. Still, I put on a brave face and no-one would have known that I spent probably one day every two weeks feeling very depressed and not knowing what to do next.

I hadn't been back working at King's Cross for many months when my great friend Don lost his job in most unfortunate circumstances. Losing him was a real blow to me, to say nothing of his wife and family, and I was left to try to pick up the pieces with the team and carry on as normal. There were some days when all I wanted to do was run away and hide.

It's difficult to explain this to anyone who hasn't worked in railway catering, but at that point in time, working on the trains was very stressful. Imagine working in a pub or restaurant where you have to go and get all the equipment you need for your working day from a store, every day, before you can start work. Then you have to find somewhere to put it. Then, quite often, you have to clean it before you can use it. It really was as if our management were conspiring to make life as difficult for us as possible. I had been looking forward to the introduction of the new electric trains on the East Coast main line, but after a few months of the expected teething problems with the new equipment, it was obvious that whoever had designed the kitchens had never worked in a kitchen or on a train in their life.

While all this was going on the management decided to re-structure the on-board staff and I was told that I was going to be a Purser instead of a Chief Steward. I would receive a bonus if my train made its financial targets, which included wastage and some customer service measures too. I was quite enthusiastic about that idea, especially as I was to get a raise in my basic salary too. I quite liked the idea of being responsible for something.

The best part of this change was that I got to go on a number of training courses. The first one was in a quality hotel in Watford, for a week. I thoroughly enjoyed the training that was delivered by a guy called Steve and his partner Susie. The whole experience was very motivational and I learned a lot. It was the first real training course that I had ever been on in my life and I had been working on the railway for over ten years at this point in time! We had people from several different departments on the railway coming to speak to us and listen to us – I had never met anyone from head office before, and it was quite obvious that most of the people who came to meet us had never met front line people before. They went away with our requests for better equipment and staffing ringing in their ears, and I was hopeful that the support we received from management might improve. We also had two days in Manchester and another two days in Wolverhampton with the same two trainers. By the end of all that training I was extremely motivated, had acquired the skills to manage a team of customer service professionals and interview potential new recruits. I couldn't wait to get back to work and start putting all my enthusiasm to work on my team.

Then reality struck. On my first day back at work after the training we had fifteen minutes to prepare our train because it had arrived late from the sidings. It took at least an hour to prepare the train properly, with linen tablecloths throughout first class and little posy bowls on each table, plus an intricate table lay-up for our 90-seater restaurant and our Silver Standard coach to prepare too. It seems difficult to believe now that we did all this with a team of seven or eight people, and that the kitchen was smaller than any kitchen I have ever seen in anyone's home.

To make matters worse, I had managers travelling with me every day, to make sure that I was making my announcements to script. You really didn't need managers under your feet when the entire team were all rushing around trying to provide the best possible service to customers in a very short time. More than once, now that we had the new, all-singing, all-dancing electric trains, we would run out of time, and I can remember several occasions when I had to drop someone off at Wakefield to collect the breakfast payments from first class customers who had got off the train there. My managers didn't have an answer to that problem, and now that I was supposed to be a manager too, I was as much in the dark as ever.

I remember spending the evenings on the training courses drinking, and socialising with the staff from other parts of the country. We found that we all had the same challenges at work and it was interesting to work with different people and see how they dealt with all the situations that occurred when trying to serve food and drink on a train that is travelling well in excess of 100 mph!

Going back to work after those courses was great, until you realised that the people you were working with, by and large, weren't as motivated as you were! I was still being expected to get a quart out of a pint pot every day, and now I had revenue targets to worry about as well. I remember practically everyone achieved their bonus in the first period, because the targets had been set low, but barely anyone achieved a bonus after that.

I had a smart new uniform that distinguished me from the rest of the staff and some of the new Pursers let the title go to their heads a bit, but I knuckled down and continued to work as part of my team, directing and supporting the others where necessary and making sure everyone felt appreciated. The novelty of being a Purser began to wear off when I realised that nothing else had changed. The support we got was minimal, and I didn't really want managers travelling on my train because they tended to get in the way and expect my staff to achieve the impossible, like standing on the platform at King's Cross welcoming passengers when the train wasn't properly prepared!

Eventually I began to find it more and more difficult to motivate myself to get up and go to work in the mornings. I quite often had sleepless nights, lying awake and wondering what I was going to be faced with at work, and worrying about how I was going to motivate the staff to, yet again, provide a service when the support we were getting from our off-train managers was almost non-existent. I think they knew what was going on, but the decision to change the way we worked had been taken very high up in the organisation and no-one dared challenge the people at the top.

One morning it all came to a head for me. I had been tossing and turning all night and had barely slept. How was I going to get through another day like the last day and the one before it?

I got up at 5 am and called in sick. I knew no-one would be in the office and that my message would be recorded on an answering machine. Let them pay me for the day for doing nothing – I deserved it. Of course, I spent the day sitting in my flat feeling guilty because I had let my team down, but there was nothing else I could do. You just didn't challenge managers on the railway in those days.

I hadn't taken more than four or five days off sick since I had been ill with cancer in 1980. Now, I took a whole month off. I called in sick again after the first week, having no idea that I was supposed to provide a medical certificate. I wasn't even registered with a doctor, although

167

a girl that I had almost had a fling with had insisted that I go to a dentist a few months before. She had been the ex-girlfriend of a friend and we had seen each other a few times before she moved back to Lancashire, where she was originally from.

During my four-week absence from work I continued with my social life, such as it was, telling my friends that I had just taken a few weeks leave that was owed to me. No-one was that close to me, and no-one questioned me. I felt extremely guilty about being away from work when there was nothing physically wrong with me, but I just couldn't face going to work in such difficult circumstances. Every day I would put off the inevitable question 'What am I going to do?' until the next day. I knew I couldn't carry on like this, but didn't know what to do for the best.

On my fourth week off sick, I was sitting in my front room watching cricket on television. It was a glorious day and I was wishing I was actually at the cricket instead of just watching it on TV. But I had not even the energy to get up and out, and buy the tickets needed. Suddenly, and completely unexpectedly, there was a ring at my front door bell followed by a very loud, authoritative knock. I went to the front window and looked out through the net curtains into the street. There was a police car parked outside the house and two big policemen standing at the door.

I went out and answered the door, blinking uncertainly in the sunlight.

'Mr Frost?' said one of the policemen.

'Yes,' I replied. I hadn't had any dealings with the police since my borstal days and they managed to make me feel like a naughty schoolboy.

'I think you should contact your employers, sir.' said the policeman. 'People are worried about you.'

'OK,' I said, 'I will call them now – thank you.'

The policeman nodded and he and his colleague turned on their heel and walked over to their car. They probably had better things to do in Brixton, in 1990, than run round after someone who was skiving off work.

I went back into the flat and looked at the phone. I suppose I had better get it over with, I thought.

I picked up the phone and dialled the number of the office at King's Cross. The call was answered by the roster clerk, who I didn't get on too well with.

'Oh. I thought you were dead,' she said. 'Are you coming back to work?'

I explained that I wasn't sure whether I was coming back to work or not, but I needed to come and talk to someone about it. Fortunately, Jane, one of the managers, was in the office and I was passed over to her. She was much more caring and sounded quite concerned. I explained that I had, in fact, called in sick twice during the past month and left messages on the answering machine in the office, but I was told that these messages hadn't been received. I said to Jane that I would like to come in and see her as soon as possible, and she agreed to see me the following afternoon.

It turned out that a great friend and colleague of mine at King's Cross had raised the alarm when he realised that I hadn't been to work for nearly a month. He had drawn this to the attention of the management and insisted that they contacted the police. I wonder how long I would have sat at home for if the police hadn't called?

The following afternoon I went to King's Cross to see Jane. I walked along Platform 8 to the stairs that went down to the offices in the basement of the station. I was thinking that this was going to be the last time that I would make this journey. I had decided that enough was enough – I was going to quit my job on the railway and look for something else. I had not discussed this with anyone, I had just gone into my shell and come up with an answer, as I normally do when I have a problem to solve.

I walked along the corridor to Jane's office and knocked on the door. I walked in and waited for Jane to finish a telephone conversation. Jane was an attractive younger woman with a caring approach to her staff.

'Jane,' I said, when she had put the phone down, 'I think I am going to have to quit my job. I don't think I can handle the pressure any more, so I have come to give you my notice.'

Jane looked at me. 'Graham,' she replied. 'You are a valued member of staff around here and I don't want to lose you. How would you feel about staying and changing over trains to an easier shift?'

I hadn't expected this, in fact, I hadn't known what to expect from the meeting. I was well-known to the management team but I had never realised that they thought that much of me.

I asked her which train she was offering me, and she told me that Jez, my friend from the Tenerife holiday of a few years earlier, had agreed to take on my train so that I could change to a quieter shift.

I sat and swallowed hard, thinking quickly. Had I really any idea of what I was going to do if I left the railway? Did I want to go back into the pub business?

I made up my mind very quickly.

'I'll take your kind offer, if I may,' I said. 'When would you like me to start?'

I agreed to start on my new train the following week, and to take some of the time off that I had had as unpaid leave. I felt relieved as I left Jane's office. I had a few more days off and then I would pull myself together and come back to work. Everything would be all right and things would soon get back to normal.

The following week I started on my new train, the 08.20 to Leeds. It was a long shift, over 15 hours a day, but because of the length of the shift I only had to work five days out of every fourteen, and no weekends. I resolved to do no overtime for a while, and to try to build my life outside work again. It was not as busy and I had less staff to supervise.

I went to a lot of jazz gigs in London during that time. It was great to lose myself in the music. I remember getting the bus from Brixton to Croydon quite often on Sunday lunchtimes to see great jazz musicians play for free in a pub there. It was a great way to escape from the realities of life for a few hours, as I had reached a point in my life where I was asking myself, 'Is this it?' I would still see my old friends in The Cricketers at The Oval cricket ground on Sundays from time to time, and I bought records by the dozen, building up a large collection of over 600 vinyl albums.

I had never learned to drive and was embarrassed to tell people that, so invented the lie that I could drive but chose not to. In any event, living in central London there was no need for a car, and with the amount of alcohol I drank, I was probably rarely sober enough to drive! I had reached a point in my life when I needed major change. I was lonely, in a city where it is easy for people to be forgotten. My life outside of work had become less fulfilling as my friends went off in their own directions, although there was one great honour I enjoyed around that time.

My friends Nick and Karen had two children by this time, and had moved to a larger house in a different Norfolk village. I was asked to be godfather to their elder daughter, and enjoyed a wonderful weekend with them and extended friends and family celebrating their daughters' christening.

I remember enjoying being the barbecue chef for a gathering of twenty or thirty on a glorious sunny day in Norfolk and staying at the local pub for the weekend with Tamsin, my co-godparent.

Nick and Karen had their own life and children now, and rightly so. I was ready for something new in my life, and something new was what I was about to get.

Chapter 14

Tina and Me

I was aware of a new female member of staff joining the team at King's Cross, and I had seen Tina in the bar of the Great Northern Hotel, where I often went for a drink after work, and thought she looked rather lively and attractive. Tina was pretty, outgoing and a lot of the guys at work were talking about her. One Saturday night I saw her in the bar of the Great Northern Hotel again, with one of the railway catering staff, Joe. It was obvious that they hadn't been working as they were smartly dressed, so I assumed that Tina was going out with Joe, and dismissed any lingering thoughts I was having about trying to find a way of asking her out.

Two weeks later I had a vacancy on my crew and noticed that Tina had been allocated to my team for the day. She turned up on the train and asked me what I wanted her to do. I asked her if she was comfortable working the buffet, and she said that she might need a bit of help with the paperwork but that she would be happy to do that job. As the morning wore on I found myself admiring her from a distance, and my old chef, Roy, remarked that I had a twinkle in my eye for her. At the end of that trip I thanked her for her work and she went on her way. We had exchanged a few words during a break and I had found out that Tina was from Peterborough, a place I had visited very early in my railway career when I had attended a colleague's wedding there. The next day I was at work, there was Tina again. This time she was working with me for all four trips and that meant working back from Bradford with me on the late evening trip, when the train was very quiet. We had the opportunity for a chat, and I found out a bit more about Tina. She was single, attractive and lived on her own in Peterborough. We shared interests in music and I found her easy to talk to. There was something that drew me to her, but at the same time there was a little voice in my head telling me not to get involved.

During that conversation Tina asked me if I had a vacancy for a permanent crew member. I told her that I did have a vacancy, and said that I would consider her for the position. Tina was quite new to the railway – that meant that she had not yet been assigned a regular crew to work with. She wanted regular shifts, and I needed someone that I could rely on and that would work hard. I wasn't about to make a decision based on two days' experience, especially as I fancied Tina. I was old enough and wise enough by then not to let my heart rule my head. At least, I thought I was. I was trying to be very dispassionate on the surface, but I knew in my heart that I was going to fall for this lady if I wasn't careful. The day finished very late, as was usual on this shift, and the pubs were closed, so I caught the tube home to Brixton thinking about Tina the whole time and wondering if anything would happen between us.

After another couple of days of working together we had chatted some more and I thought she was too good to be true. Just over two years older than me, Tina was vivacious, funny, flirtatious and pretty. She gave the impression that she would be the life and soul of a party. Outside work, she said she enjoyed parties, live music and enjoyed a drink and a smoke, of both varieties. The second week we worked together, I asked her out. My plan was to take her to a restaurant in Covent Garden, and we arranged our date for the following Saturday, when we were both off work. Saturday arrived and I received a phone call from Tina in the afternoon.

'I'm really sorry, I can't make it down to London tonight,' she said, 'because I'm invited to a birthday party in Peterborough. It's a woman I used to work with and I'd really like to go, so would you like to come to that with me?'

I hummed and hawed for a whole second, then agreed to catch a train up to Peterborough and go to the party with her. Tina had also said that I could stay at her place for the night, so I was understandably quite enthusiastic, although there was still a questioning voice in the back of my mind. Tina picked me up in a taxi at Peterborough station and we went to her friend's party, where we danced the night away and hardly spoke to anyone else. By the end of the evening we were slow-dancing and I was feeling very good indeed. We took another taxi back to Tina's house in another part

179

of Peterborough – it was about 2am. Tina made us some coffee, then snuggled up to me on the sofa.

After a few moments she looked at me and said, 'I'm not going to sleep with you tonight because I don't want you to think I'm easy.'

I was quite happy about that because, even at the advanced age of 34, I had never had a one-night stand, and had, in fact, never slept with a woman on a first date at that time. We made out a bit on the sofa, listened to a variety of music, and I'm not sure if either of us ever went to bed. I remember Tina saying to me that she felt safe with me, and I wondered what she meant by that. There were all sorts of questions going around my mind, as this sort of thing just never happened to me. Here was an attractive, sexy, lively woman who wanted to be with me! Of course, I had always struggled with my own self-esteem and I wondered what she saw in me. I must have slept at some point because I remember being woken up with a cup of tea and breakfast. On the Sunday we went to the pub at lunchtime, where a live band was playing. It was exactly what I would have been doing if I was at home in London on a Sunday, except that here I was with an attractive woman who seemed to really want to be with me.

We met some of Tina's friends at the pub – a couple called Dave and Sally. Dave and I talked about music and found that we both liked Prefab Sprout, a popular band of the time. Dave was a few years older than me and a really great guy. It transpired that he had been out with Tina in the past, but it hadn't worked out for them and he was now living with her friend Sally. He was a builder and Sally ran a catering business. After the pub, Sally dropped us back at Tina's house in her van. I dread to think how much alcohol had been consumed but Sally was still driving. One of the reasons I felt comfortable with these people was because they drank as much as, possibly more than, I did.

When we arrived back at Tina's house she sat me in front of the television and disappeared into the kitchen, re-appearing no more than fifteen minutes later with a massive roast chicken dinner, which she had prepared before we went out, complete with wine. It was the first weekend we had spent together but I was hooked!

Tina was the first woman I had met who had a proper hi-fi system and a large record and CD collection. That played a big part in my interest in her. There was also a beguiling combination of vulnerability and vivacity that I began to find totally irresistible. I felt like a small insect that was floating in a bath when someone pulled the plug out – what was happening to me was almost beyond my control. It was totally different from how I had felt when I was with my first serious girlfriend, Anne, in the 1970s, but I had a similar feeling of not really being in control. Perhaps I was bewitched. I certainly ignored that little voice from my heart that was telling me to be careful.

I was fortunate to be working a shift where I was off every weekend. This was unheard of on the railway and I was determined to enjoy it as much as possible. Tina invited me up to Peterborough on the weekend after our first date and took me out to meet some more of her friends. They all seemed to spend a lot of their time in the pub, which was fine by me in those days. We did sleep together that second weekend but the physical side was not great between us. That was probably because I was lacking in confidence in that area since my encounter with cancer a few years previously. I had not had a regular relationship that had lasted any length of time since Anne and I had separated in 1981. However, I really enjoyed being with Tina and thought that the physical side of the relationship would work itself out eventually. We never really talked about this part of the relationship. Tina was aware of my past history and the fact that I had suffered from testicular cancer in the past. It was as if neither of us really wanted to broach the subject.

Tina did spend a weekend with me in London during the first few weeks that we were together. She was not keen to meet my friends and it was obvious that she preferred us to spend the weekends in Peterborough where she was more in her comfort zone. I was happy to go along with that as I enjoyed her company and liked most of her friends. There was one sticking point early on in the relationship. Tina was very keen on shopping and treated it as a recreation. She would think nothing of going off into Peterborough city centre quite early on a Saturday morning and embarking on a shopping expedition that would quite often last until late afternoon. As her new and supportive boyfriend I went along with this for a couple of Saturdays, but then realised that these shopping trips were not really for me and managed to stay at Tina's home watching television, listening to music or reading while she went shopping with one or two of her female friends.

Chapter 15

More about Tina

It was during one of the shopping trips that I went on with Tina that I was introduced to her daughter. Tina had told me that she had a 14-year old daughter from her failed marriage several years previously. The first time I met Hannah I was shocked. She was a punk, dressed in leather trousers and chains, with tattoos and piercings. Tina explained me that her daughter lived away from home because she couldn't control her. When I met Hannah I immediately understood. A little voice in my head did ask me how someone could end up with a daughter like that, because I realised that 14-year old girls are not all as angry with life as Hannah obviously was, but very early on in our relationship I developed a habit of ignoring the little voice in my head where Tina was concerned. I accepted what she recounted to me, albeit with some secret doubts.

Tina would often fix me with a loving gaze and just tell me that she was 'so happy' with me and felt so safe, that all my doubts would melt away. People at work had seen us together and I was careful to ensure that our personal relationship did not get in the way of us working together. Our friends at work joked that everyone knew we were seeing each other before we did, because we were both so secretive about our growing fondness for each other, and would deny that we were seeing each other if anyone asked.

One day at work, Tina was sitting down while everyone else on the team, including me, was still working. I asked her why she was sitting down when there was still work to do.

'Aren't there any perks for being the Chief Steward's girlfriend, then? asked Tina, with a cheeky look.

'No, there aren't,' I replied, quite angrily. I was determined that our out-of-work relationship was not going to change anything at work. There was an unwritten rule on the railway at the time that people who were married or in a

186

relationship shouldn't work together, and I didn't want to fall foul of that.

That weekend I spoke to Tina about how I felt she was taking advantage of our relationship while we were at work.

'Does that mean we are a couple then?' she asked, and snuggled up to me. She really was quite irresistible but I was determined that my reputation for fairness and honesty at work was not going to get tarnished. After a few weeks I decided that we needed to work on different trains, and I was able to organise for Tina to work a different train, but mostly the same days as me, so that we could still spend a lot of time together.

In many ways, Tina was ideal for me. She enjoyed a drink, smoked and liked to have an active social life, mainly around pubs and live music. She had a lot of friends in Peterborough as she had lived there for most of her life. Tina had been born in Peterborough two-and-a-half years before I was born. Her mother had originally been from Manchester, and had retired back to the North West a few years before Tina and I met. Tina's father had passed away when she was very young. She had a few old black and white photos of him but didn't speak of him very often. I formed the impression that Tina had not had a very happy early life. Tina went to great lengths to tell me all about her personal life before she had met me. It appeared that she had suffered from quite low self-esteem for most of her life and that this had led her to have a number of short-lived, abusive relationships with men. She could be one of the most frustrating and difficult people to be with, and then she would suddenly metamorphose into this wonderful person who said that she loved me and felt safe with me. I resolved to try and help her to feel better about herself and be the happy person that I thought she deserved to be.

We had only been seeing each other for about six weeks when she announced that we were going up to Manchester for the weekend to meet her mother. I felt a little awkward about this but went along with it just to keep Tina happy. I had told her about my family background. At that time, it had been many years since I had heard from my family and I had a feeling that they wouldn't have been terribly impressed with my latest choice of girlfriend. We travelled up to Manchester on the train and one of Tina's aunts picked us up from the station and took us to Tina's mother's tiny house in a village on the outskirts of Manchester. We had to sleep on a mattress on the living room floor which was interesting to say the least, as neither of us were small people! Tina's mother, who was in her sixties, seemed to take to me and was very welcoming and friendly. I found out where Tina had inherited her penchant for shopping from, as her mother never seemed happier than when she was mooching around shops or a market. I suffered in silence as they flitted from one shop or market stall to another, completely oblivious to the fact that I was there, frustratedly walking a few paces behind them, trying unsuccessfully to conceal my boredom.

Eventually, I succumbed. 'Tina, would you like that dress you tried on back there, the red one?' I asked.

'Why, are you going to buy it for me – it's ever so expensive?' she replied.

The dress was about £50, quite a lot of money in 1991, but it was worth it to see the look on her face. Unfortunately, she only ever wore it once as she decided that it made her look too big.

The few days in the North West came to an end when we went out for a meal with some of Tina's elderly relatives and I felt as if they wanted me to be part of their family. One of her aunts confided in me that she had never brought a boyfriend up there before and her mother obviously approved of me too. I was beginning to be absorbed into her family as well as being hooked by Tina herself.

After our trip to Manchester I spent more and more time in Peterborough with Tina. One weekend we invited Dave and Sally down to London for the weekend. We all went to Brixton Academy on the Saturday night to see Ian Dury and the Blockheads, one of my favourite live bands of the 1980s, and on the Sunday lunchtime we went to a pub, the Half Moon in Herne Hill, to see a local band perform. I remember being quite proud that I had such brilliant live music literally within walking distance of where I lived, but I got the impression that Tina felt a bit like a fish out of water in London and was much more comfortable with me going up to Peterborough to be with her.

Perhaps this was because Tina had unhappy memories of having lived in London briefly during her marriage several years before I met her. She had married a man who was a little older than her and he had taken her to live in Balham. They had their daughter Hannah there, and when Hannah was still quite a small child, Tina had taken her back to Peterborough, leaving her husband in London. I could never get Tina to speak about the relationship with her husband, so I decided not to press her on the subject. Tina also had a half-sister and a niece who lived in Surrey. Soon after we had been to Manchester to meet Tina's mother, we spent a weekend in Surrey with Tina's niece and her husband. I didn't feel any great affinity with them, feeling that they looked down on us a little as they appeared to be quite wealthy. Tina was not speaking to her half-sister at this point in time so I was spared the pleasure of meeting her. I was able to understand her position due to the fact that I had barely spoken to anyone in my family for over fifteen years.

I hadn't been seeing Tina for very long when she found out that her daughter, Hannah, was pregnant. I had only met Hannah once or twice, and she had never been to Tina's house when I was there, so I had almost managed to convince myself that she wasn't anyone for me to worry about, but I couldn't help but be a little curious about it was that she did not live at home when she was still only just over fifteen years of age. I had, very early in our relationship, come to the realisation that Tina only spoke about what she wanted to speak about, so I decided to be supportive and not ask questions. My 'inner voice' was saying 'Oh my goodness, whatever is going to happen next?' but I ignored it because I was on a roller-coaster as far as Tina was concerned. I was going to make this work, come what may. Apparently, Hannah was adamant that she was going to keep the baby. I just listened and made what I hoped were appropriate noises while Tina spent the day of the discovery crying, composing herself, wanting to talk and not wanting to talk. I was completely out of my depth with the situation but reasoned with myself that I had to try to rescue it in any way that I could. Tina went to her best friend Sally's house and poured out her heart to Sally while

I listened. I took Tina to the local pub for lunch to try to take her mind off the situation but nothing seemed to work. Tina was quite obviously not looking forward to becoming a grandmother when she was still eighteen months short of her fortieth birthday.

I saw little or nothing of Hannah during her pregnancy and decided that least said, soonest mended was the most appropriate approach to the whole situation where I was concerned. I was determined to make things work with Tina; after all, here I was, thirty-five years of age and still single. No-one had really showed any great interest in me for several years and now here was Tina. She seemed to need me and said she loved me. It wasn't a perfect relationship, but it was worth working on, as far as I was concerned.

Chapter 15

Deeper and Deeper

After Tina and I had been seeing each other for a few months, we decided to go on holiday together. It was a big step for me, as I had never been away for more than a long weekend with a girlfriend before, and here I was thinking of going away with a woman for a whole fortnight. We settled on Tunisia, for no better reason than that neither of us had been there before, and it was an exotic destination. I had paid for the entire holiday on the understanding that Tina would repay me when we returned from Tunisia. I told myself that I was enjoying being with her so there was nothing wrong with paying for her to go on holiday.

The time for our holiday in Tunisia came, and we set off to Gatwick Airport. This was at the same time as the first Gulf War ended and we were probably the first plane-load of British tourists to arrive in Tunisia after the ceasefire. To say that we received a warm welcome there would be an overstatement. Our tour operator representative suggested that we should avoid going out of our hotel in the evenings and asked us to be very careful where we went in the daytime. That meant that we were confined to the hotel bar in the evenings, where the main activity was playing bingo. As Tunisia is a Muslim country alcohol is not freely available. What alcoholic drinks are available are mostly imported and very expensive. That was the only holiday I had ever been on where I ran out of money and had to resort to using a credit card.

Tina and I mostly really enjoyed each other's company. We had decided that Van Morrison's 'Have I Told You Lately...?' was 'our song' and I remember one night in bed listening to that song through one headphone each from a Walkman cassette player and singing it to each other. Tina loved to sunbathe, and the weather was really hot and ideal for sun worshippers, so she was happy with that. I told myself that I was happy as long as she was happy. I was beginning to realise that being with someone like Tina involved quite a lot of running around after her. She was an attractive woman and seemed to particularly appeal to the

Tunisian men. The expression *Bees round a honey-pot* springs to mind. It was almost impossible for me to leave her by the pool at our hotel for more than five minutes without her being surrounded by two or three swarthy local men. I don't really think she did much to discourage them as she would always have a big smirk on her face when I returned with a drink or a snack for her.

During our two weeks in Tunisia Tina made friends with an English girl, Shirley, who lived out there with her Tunisian boyfriend. They went shopping together a couple of times and Tina suddenly decided that she wanted to move to Tunisia. She suggested that we buy a karaoke machine and move out together to start a karaoke business around the Tunisian hotels. I had learned enough about Tina by now to know that it was best not to shoot her ideas down in flames, so I said I would think about it. The truth was that there was no way I was going to give up a secure job at home to move out there to an uncertain future, just because the sun shone a lot in Tunisia. I was to learn that Tina was fond of coming up with hare-brained ideas without thinking them through, something I found

196

frustrating and endearing in equal measure as our relationship progressed.

While we were in Tunisia we took a two-day trip into the Sahara Desert. I remember arriving in the Sahara in a coach, and having to wait for the rain to stop before we got off the coach and went into the hotel that we were booked into for the night. It struck me that this was the last place on earth that you would expect to find rain, perhaps on a par with arriving at the North Pole in the middle of a heatwave. Nevertheless, it was raining in the Sahara Desert when we arrived there. The hotel we stayed in there was of a much higher standard than the one where we spent the rest of our holiday, which I enjoyed. We had a try at riding a camel while we were there, which was a most uncomfortable experience for me and, by all accounts, a very enjoyable experience for Tina.

Another memorable experience on this holiday was taking a ride on an old-fashioned Tunisian train with a stateroom on board in which we spent part of the journey. A busman's holiday, I suppose, but it was interesting to see their railway as it was so much a part of my life. I also remember visiting Tunis, the capital city, and being asked for money when I wanted to take a picture of a group of elderly men sitting on a bench by a fruit stall. I'm afraid I didn't pay, but I still managed to take the picture. I had little concept, in those days, of the poverty in which people lived in some parts of the world. Working on the railway, I was protected from reality in many ways. We got a pay increase every year, there was always plenty of overtime available, and we enjoyed a very good lifestyle compared to many other people.

Tina fully indulged her passion for shopping in Tunisia. She particularly enjoyed bargaining for goods in the local markets and went off for a couple of hours most days with her new friend Shirley. By the time we got to the end of our fortnight, the spare single bed in our hotel room was groaning under the weight of Tina's purchases and she had to buy an extra suitcase to pack everything into when we returned home. All in all, I enjoyed my first holiday with Tina; although I found some parts of her personality and behaviour difficult to deal with I was falling for her in a big way. I was becoming more prepared to forgive her little idiosyncrasies, some of which I found quite adorable. We had not yet had a major argument, largely because I had got into the habit of backing down to avoid confrontation, and the physical side of our relationship was still not satisfactory for either of us. All in all, our relationship was a disaster waiting to happen, but we continued blindly on with it as we both felt we had something of worth in each other.

I had generally neglected my other friends in the few months that I had been seeing Tina. Having a girlfriend in Peterborough where I would spend every weekend meant that the time spent with Mel and my other London friends suffered. Tina was not at all concerned about that and I was insufficiently assertive to stand up to her, so gradually her friends became my new friends. I liked Dave and Sally – the four of us became 'groupies' for a very good band called Crescendo World who were popular in the Peterborough area in the early 1990's. They based their material on bands like Steely Dan, Prefab Sprout and REM, and we must have gone to see them at least twenty times over a period of a few months. There was a dearth of quality music in Peterborough, especially for someone like me who was used to the London music scene, but these Crescendo World guys were top musicians and very good to listen to.

Tina had some other friends that I gradually started to meet. There was Coral, who lived with her daughters in a large house in another part of Peterborough, and who seemed never to have done a day's work in her life. I had heard that there were people who had lived on benefits for their entire lives, but I had never really believed that this sort of culture existed. I had only ever been on the dole for a week in my life, and by the time I had received my first dole cheque, back in the late 1970s, I had found another job. Some of Tina's friends seemed to have rarely, if ever, been in work. I kept all my doubts to myself, but I was beginning to realise that I had a lot on my hands in our relationship. However, I have never been a quitter, and I liked being with Tina most of the time, so I swallowed my questions and put on a brave and happy face.

Chapter 16

Leo

Tina became a grandmother in the late summer of 1991. Leo was born very prematurely and it was touch and go whether he would survive. Tina's daughter, Hannah, had not looked after herself terribly well during her pregnancy, during which she had mostly lived in council care. I had kept out of the situation, largely because Tina didn't want to talk about it. I had learned very early on in the relationship that if Tina didn't want to talk about something, we didn't talk about it. At the same time, if she suddenly decided that she did want to open up about something, it would be very much on the agenda, but only until she decided that it was off limits again. Tina and I were at the maternity unit when Leo was born. She was with her daughter and I waited nervously in the waiting room for several hours. Tina eventually appeared and said that we should go to the nearby pub and wet the baby's head. We went and had a few drinks. I was totally out of my depth at this point, never having been a parent, or even come remotely close to parenthood. I was now going out with someone who was grandmother to a three-month premature child by a daughter who had only just turned sixteen. There was quite a loud voice in my head at this point telling me that I should get out of there and run as far away from the situation as possible, but I had never been great at listening to the sensible voice in my head, and decided to ignore it on that occasion. I liked being needed.

Tina was quite adamant that she wasn't having Hannah and the baby home to live with her, and that life was going to go on as normal. Leo's father had not been identified at that stage, although his identity did come to light before much longer. I spent a couple of nights at my neglected flat in Brixton in the immediate aftermath of Leo's arrival, trying to get my head around the turn my life was taking. When I wasn't with Tina I missed her, and when I was with her I kept wondering what I was getting myself into. It was as if she had an invisible magnetism for me, perhaps even a destructive magnetism.

I went up to Peterborough again for the following weekend, and on the Saturday I went to the hospital with Tina to see Leo in the Special Care Baby Unit. I remember Coral, one of Tina's friends, arriving to see him and walking into the SCBU quite drunk in the middle of the afternoon and shouting, quite inappropriate behaviour for a hospital. I was horrified. Everything changed when I saw Leo for the first time. He was barely the weight of a bag of sugar, and looked like a tiny chicken lying there hooked up to all sorts of monitors and drips. I resolved immediately that I would do everything in my power to look after him and help him to have a decent chance in life, if he survived. This was literally a life-changing moment. I realised that I was, perhaps, the only truly responsible person that little Leo had in his life. I could not just walk away from the situation.

Tina was at the hospital a lot seeing Leo and Hannah for the next few weeks. She was starting to have time off work because of the situation and I was being asked questions about her condition as I was now 'officially' known as her boyfriend. The whole situation with Leo coming into our lives had changed everything. Tina was sure that Hannah wouldn't be able to care for Leo properly and she began to talk about going for custody of him herself. At the same time I asked myself the question, very silently, whether she was any more capable of looking after a child now than she had been when Hannah was young. I had begun to hear stories from some of Tina's so-called friends about how Hannah had been neglected when she was a child, and how Tina had gone out for whole weekends and left Hannah alone. I didn't dare confront Tina with this, and tried to persuade myself that people were making the stories up just to put me off her. Even Sally, who was supposed to be Tina's best friend, had warned me that she might be too much for me to handle. Still I refused to listen. I knew best, even though the voice in my head was frequently telling me to stop before I went too far. I chose to ignore it.

Little Leo was eventually allowed to leave hospital six weeks after he was born. He and his mother went to live in a family care unit run by the local council and Hannah attended child care classes. She was no more than a child herself. She would occasionally come around to her mother's house when I was there, or we would meet her in town for a coffee. I formed the impression that she was not in a very good place at all. I remember being quite thankful for the upbringing that I had experienced myself in the church – at least I had been cared for. This was a whole new experience for me and there were surprises all the time. Leo was a beautiful child and I often wondered how something so wonderful could have come about in such a strange and dysfunctional way. It transpired that his father, who was a few years older than Hannah, had been seeing Hannah on and off for quite a few years and there were suspicions that sexual relations had started between them when Hannah had been very young. Tina, inevitably, was extremely angry when she found this out. I had to stop her from going to this man's place of work and physically attacking him. It wasn't easy to stop Tina from doing something when she had her heart set on it. I was constantly discovering new extremes of being out of my depth. I had never experienced anything like it before; at times it was like being in some kind of strange movie with no script, where things just kept getting stranger. I felt that I had to stay on board for Leo's sake, and wondered, too,

205

what Tina would do without me. She would often tell me that she didn't know what she would do without me, so I guess being, at least apparently, needed was what kept me going.

After a comparatively short time out of hospital, we received the news one day that Leo had been taken away from Hannah and put in the care of foster parents. There were a lot of officials in and out of Tina's house at this time and it was all very confusing and concerning.

Apparently, Hannah had gone out with Leo one night and had not returned until the following morning. Leo had not been fed, and the powers that be had decided that this was sufficient grounds for putting Leo into foster care. I was completely out of my depth as I had no experience of anything like this. It was something that happened to other people, as far as I was concerned. I didn't see Hannah at all during this period: Tina was very involved with the authorities and went to see Leo a number of times at his foster parents', a couple in another part of Peterborough. Tina spent a lot of time in tears and I would try to console her and take her mind off the problems by offering to take her out. I was still working full time and spending almost every night at Tina's, just returning to London once a week to make sure my flat was still intact. Neither Tina nor I had a car at this point, so I was spending a lot of money running around in taxis to see different people and try to sort this rather desperate situation out. I was practically keeping Tina going financially and eating into my savings to keep things afloat.

Tina had a friend in London, Donna, whom she had met through working on the railway, and she decided to go and spend a day or two in East London with Donna to get away from everything for a while.

I had a long weekend off and went and spent it in Brixton. I spent most of that weekend sitting and thinking about what I was going to do. My new life was exciting and unpredictable but was it what I really wanted? I knew I needed to make some changes in my life, but were these really the changes that I was looking for? Should I just walk away now while I still could? All these questions went round and round in my mind for the entire weekend. I couldn't talk about it with my friends, because I knew that,

without exception, they would tell me to walk away.
People at work who had known me for years had started
giving me quizzical looks and my social life after work had
stopped entirely. All I could think about when I finished
work was what time the next train to Peterborough was and
I was drinking less than I had for a long time, although
probably smoking more!

Chapter 17

Is it over?

Soon after our weekend spent apart, Tina and I were scheduled to work together one Friday. Almost unbelievably, our train was cancelled, and we were sent home. This was an extremely rare occurrence on the railway – it only happened to me twice in the entire time I worked there, so I was determined to make the most of it. I suggested to Tina that we went and had some breakfast together so that we could talk about what we were going to do with the time that we had suddenly been given.

'Actually,' she said, 'Can we just go our separate ways today? I just want to think things through a bit, I fancy a day on my own.'

I reluctantly agreed, suggesting that I call her later and see if she wanted me to come up for the weekend. She agreed, but I could see that her mind was somewhere else, so I set off for my own home. Strangely, life in my flat in Brixton had become quite boring since I had known Tina. With her in my life, there was always something going on, even if it was difficult to deal with at times. Most of my London friends had moved on, settled down, got married and now had lives outside of the group of friends that I had been part of. I had been part of the dispersal too, because since I had met Tina I had hardly seen any of my other friends. Being Tina's boyfriend was a full time job.

It was mid-morning on Friday when I got home. I couldn't settle, wondering why Tina had decided to spend the day on her own. I thought there was something going on, but I couldn't put my finger on what it was. I called her house after a couple of hours, but there was no answer. After a while I called my old friend Jez. We had worked together on the charter trains a few years previously and had been on holiday together. He was now married to the girl he had met on that holiday and lived near Wimbledon. He had the day off work that day and readily agreed to meet me in his local pub for a pint. I caught the bus over and we sat in the bar reminiscing about old times. I brought him up to speed with events concerning Tina and me, and then told him that

I was uneasy about something and that I had decided that I needed to sort it out once and for all that day. I had enjoyed a few pints by that time and was quite fired up!

'I'm going to go up there and sort it out with her now,' I said. I had worked it all out in my mind, I would catch a train to Peterborough, go to Tina's house and confront her, and ask her what was going on that she didn't want to spend the day with me. Jez could see that I was determined, so he went along with my idea. I finished my pint and went out to catch the bus back home to Brixton. I packed an overnight bag and set off for King's Cross to catch a train up to Peterborough arriving in the city soon after 6pm. I decided to walk from the station to Tina's house, a distance of about two miles. There were several pubs en route and I stopped in two or three of them for a quick pint on my way to the confrontation. By the time I arrived at her house I had worked myself up into a terrible state. I let myself in to the house and quickly realised that there was no-one in. I helped myself to a beer from the fridge, poured it into a glass and put the empty can in the bin. While the bin was open I noticed that there was an empty vodka bottle on top of the rest of the rubbish. I hadn't seen that particular brand of vodka in the house before - it looked for all the world as if Tina had polished off an entire bottle of vodka and then gone out somewhere. I decided to stay in the house and see if she returned. I wasn't sure what I was going to say or do if she did come back, but I was determined to have it out with her. I had completely convinced myself that there was something going on, and I had to know what was happening.

I watched some television and probably made myself something to eat. At about 11.30 pm I realised that Tina was probably out somewhere and not very likely to be home any time soon. I had had another few cans of beer by this time and was feeling sleepy, so decided to go to sleep in Tina's bed. I must have gone to sleep at about midnight, and at 1.30 am I was awoken by the sound of someone coming into the house. I was sure that I heard more than one voice, and after a few seconds, everything went quiet. I guessed that Tina had realised that I was in the house. I had left my shoes on the floor in the living room, and she would have noticed them. After a few moments I got out of bed, pulled on my jeans and top, and set off downstairs to investigate what was going on. As soon as I entered the living room I saw Tina sitting there looking rather dishevelled, and then on the armchair I saw this guy who, at first glance, looked like a tramp. He had long, unruly hair, an unkempt beard going grey around the edges and my first thought was that she had picked him up off the street somewhere.

'This is Tom,' said Tina, unable to look at me. 'We've kind of been friends for a few weeks. We met in London. He's a friend of Donna's.'

'So you mean you're seeing each other?' I asked.

'Well, not exactly... well, yes, sort of...' replied Tina, still unable to look at me. 'I'm sorry.'

I just looked at the guy, completely unable to understand what Tina could see in him. He was as much unlike me as it was possible to be. The sudden realisation hit me that perhaps this was really the sort of guy that she usually went for, and perhaps it was me that was the unusual one. I thought quickly.

'Right,' I said, 'I'm going to go for a walk for ten minutes and I want you two to have a chat about whether you are really serious about each other. When I come back, you, Tom – you will go for a walk for ten minutes and Tina and I can have a chat. At the end of that time, Tina, you have to make a decision, here and now, because I'm not sharing you with him.'

I walked out of the door. I reflected that my life had become so wrapped up with Tina over the past few months that I had not had a life of my own at all. However, I wasn't ready to give up. I believed that I could help her and make her happy. I went for a ten-minute walk around the block, willing her to choose me. I really couldn't see how there could be any contest. There I was, with a good job, time and money to lavish on her – surely she wouldn't choose him over me. I arrived back at the house and after some persuasion, managed to get Tom to go for a walk. He was considerably drunker than I was and really didn't know what to say, but eventually he staggered out of the door.

When he was gone I asked Tina what on earth she was thinking of.

'Well, I don't usually go for nice blokes like you,' she replied. 'He's more my type really, rough and ready, you know?'

'Well, your life doesn't have to be like that anymore, Tina,' I said. 'You have me, what could you possibly want with him?'

She told me that she thought she loved him, and asked me to give her some time to decide.

I decided to go back to bed, and leave them to talk to each other. Tom had returned after just a few minutes and I realised that it could be over between Tina and I. Maybe I couldn't rescue her from herself after all. How could I compete with the guy? He didn't look as if he had two pennies to rub together, he needed a good bath, and yet she would rather be with him than me. I was dumbfounded. After a short, fitful sleep I waited until I knew there would be a train back to London and, after packing my few

215

belongings that had found their way to Tina's house over the past few weeks, I made my way sadly back to London. I was still sure that she would come to her senses and come back to me. I was sure that it wasn't over, but I knew I was going to have to let her work that out for herself.

With Tina suddenly no longer in my life I had a lot of time to fill. I had pretty much let her take over my life, to the detriment of my other friendships. Dave and Sally called me and let me know how sorry they were to hear how things had turned out, but otherwise I was left feeling rather lonely. It was getting quite close to Christmas and I realised that I might be spending the holiday alone. As usual, I turned to work when life got tough, because when I was at work I could forget what else was, or wasn't, going on in my life. I started working overtime again.

Chapter 18

Alone again!

I realised that I wasn't getting over Tina at all when a colleague from work asked me in passing one day how Tina was. I almost burst into tears as I told him that we weren't together any more. I couldn't carry on like that. One day I was working a train that involved being in Edinburgh for three hours. I knew Tina was working a train that went through Edinburgh while my train was there. Yes, I'm afraid I was checking out her roster to see where she was. I stood near the platform where her train was due to see if I could catch a glimpse of her. I did so more than once!

There was no denying that Tina had livened up my life tremendously, but she had also taken it over almost completely, so that I was left feeling like a fish out of water without her. I rang my old friend Mel to see what he was up to. We went for a drink or two one night and it was almost like old times. I hadn't seen much of him for a year or so. He was seeing a much younger girl that he had met while on one of his walking trips to Cornwall and was feeling quite guilty that she thought far more of him than he did of her. He was in his early forties and she was in her mid-twenties. I had seen them together once or twice before and she seemed like a really lovely girl. I couldn't see what he was moaning about! We started talking about Christmas, and Mel said that he was not relishing the idea of spending Christmas with his girlfriend's parents. I suggested that we do something for Christmas and we ended up booking a cottage together in St. Just, Cornwall for a few days.

I will always remember that trip to Cornwall. It was the third time Mel and I had been to Cornwall together, and the first time during winter. We found a pleasant little pub in St. Just, just up the road from our rented cottage, and sank a few pints of the local Tinner's ale on Christmas Eve, after a long walk on the coastal path. I remember eating roast duck on Christmas Day, and washing it down with a good few glasses of red wine. I was beginning to acquire a taste for red wine at this time in my life, something that has stayed with me. I was unable to completely erase Tina from my mind during the Christmas break, but I knew what Mel would say if I tried to discuss it with him, so I kept my thoughts to myself. I knew that my deep feelings for Tina were really not reciprocated and that she was trouble, but I was unable to stop myself thinking that I could help her to be happy.

On Boxing Day, Mel and I decided to walk around the coast path from St. Just to Land's End. I had memories of having been to Land's End as a child. We had had a photograph taken of all the Frost family at the Land's End signpost, and I hadn't been back there since. I was disappointed to see that it had turned into a so-called tourist paradise, and there were quite a number of people there for a Boxing Day. Mel and I had some lunch there and then, after resting for an hour or so, we set off to walk back the way we had come, along the coast path. The distance from Land's End back to St. Just was about eight miles by the coast path so we figured we would have walked about fifteen miles on the day, a good day's walking. Shortly after we set off a thick fog enveloped us and we were forced to turn back and take the much longer option of walking back by road. By the time we trudged wearily into the pub in St. Just we had walked over twenty miles in a day. I had been quiet during most of the walk as I was still turning the events of the past few weeks over in my mind. I was not able to erase Tina from my mind, despite the long walks and convivial eating and drinking. She stayed in my mind, no matter what I was doing, or who I was with.

I returned to work during the week between Christmas and New Year. It is a strange time of year on the railway as there was a special timetable and none of the trains had restaurants, so we would often work different shifts and work with unknown people . One day I was working with a girl that I knew a little.

'I hear your Tina's not too happy with her new fella,' said Margaret, the girl I was working with.

When I asked her what she meant, it appeared that someone else at King's Cross had given Tina a lift home

220

after work one night and Tina had not wanted to go in to her own house. I assumed that she had moved Tom into the house with her and he was now giving her a hard time. I knew that I should keep well away from the situation but I also knew how I still felt about Tina. There was unfinished business there and I knew that I could rescue her from the situation that she had got herself into and make her happy again.

What was only a few days between public holidays seemed to go on forever. There wasn't any overtime available at work and the friends that I had left in London were all out of town. I couldn't talk to Mel about the situation with Tina as I knew what he would say. All my friends would have told me to forget about her and run as far away from her as possible, if they knew what was going on. However, and not for the first time in my life, I ignored everyone's advice, including my own.

Tina eventually rang me during the New Year break. She asked if she could come down and see me, and I invited her to come down that night.

'I have made a terrible mistake' she said, looking very downcast and humble. 'Can we just go back to how things were?'

After some discussion I agreed that I would get back together with her, but that she would have to get rid of Tom. Tina said that he had moved in with her the day after I had found them together, and that he had not done a day's work since, nor looked for a job, and that he had been living off her and scrounging money off her to go to the pub. If she refused, he was threatening her with violence. I knew that this was far from the first time that Tina had been involved with a violent man. We discussed the situation long into the night. It had been complicated even more by the fact that Tina had decided to apply for custody of little Leo, her grandson, and she felt that the situation with Tom would compromise any chance she had of getting Leo to come and live with her. The authorities had decided that her daughter, Hannah, was not capable of looking after him at that time, and the only alternative was long-term foster care or adoption. Hannah was not in favour of either of those options, but had apparently been persuaded that her mother might be able to look after Leo until Hannah was in a proper state to look after him herself again.

I reminded myself of my unspoken pledge to Leo when he was first born. I had decided that I would do everything I could to make sure that he had a decent start in life. The pieces of this bizarre jigsaw were beginning to come together in life-changing symmetry. I could do something really worthwhile by taking care of Tina and Leo. Everything would be all right and two people's lives would be sorted out. I was thinking that I had found a good reason for rescuing Tina from Tom and that everything would work out for the best. There were big doubts in my mind, but I pushed them to one side. I had decided on my course of action and nothing would dissuade me from it now.

Chapter 19

The Big Decision

The following week I took Tina to my favourite restaurant in Covent Garden and asked her to marry me. She accepted straight away, and we decided to get married in August, which was eight months away. I remember us travelling up to Peterborough together the next day. Tom had only just moved out of her house and Leo was living with foster parents a couple of miles away. Tina had to go and see him practically every day as part of the bonding process prior to him coming to live with her. Hannah had decided to fight the residence order so lawyers had to be found and funded. I agreed to fund the court case and was taken to meet the family law solicitor. It was agreed that I would pay a deposit and then a monthly amount until the full legal bill was settled. It was likely to be over a thousand pounds. I remember thinking to myself that I was 'in for a penny, in for a pound'. There was no escape now!

Somehow, Tina and I found time to go and buy her an engagement ring from a jeweller's shop in Peterborough city centre. That put a smile on her face and left me with a bill for £400, but I was past caring. I was on the roller coaster ride that was to completely change my life over the next few months. I felt rather like someone who was on a runaway train and had no idea where the brakes were. That little voice in my head was asking me all sorts of questions about what I was getting mixed up in, but I really couldn't find the 'off' switch, and wasn't sure if I wanted to. If I had walked away at that point Leo would almost certainly have stayed in foster care and probably been adopted, and I felt that I couldn't stand by and watch that happen. I also cared for Tina enough to want to help her have a happier life. Not for the first time in my life, I found myself at the bottom of my own list of priorities.

Over the next few weeks, I found myself spending nearly all my time in Peterborough. I was practically keeping two homes going, as all Tina's income seemed to be going on baby clothes and equipment. We had no car, so a lot of money was also being spent on taxis. Tina said that if I bought a car she could drive it, and I asked her if she had ever passed her driving test.

'Well, no,' she said, 'but I've driven, loads of times.'

I had never driven a car in my life, apart from a brief stab at driving a stolen Austin Cambridge many years earlier. I realised that if we were going to have a child living with us, we were going to need a car. I decided that we would both have driving lessons, and that I would pay for that too. The son of some friends had a rather beaten-up old Ford Fiesta for sale, so I bought that and put it into storage ready for the day when one of us passed our driving test.

I decided that if I was going to be a surrogate father for a small child, my lifestyle was going to have to change. I hoped that if Tina saw me changing my ways, she would be influenced by that and would calm down herself. I practically stopped drinking and cut down on smoking considerably. I would finish work and catch the first train back to Peterborough, rather than going to the pub after work.

We were visited by an assortment of officials, all of whom were tasked with ensuring that we were offering little Leo a stable home where he would be looked after properly. To give Tina credit, she really tried very hard. I think she saw having Leo as an opportunity to get something right. Underneath all her bravado there was a very genuine person trying to get out, and I saw flashes of that person quite regularly when there were just the two of us together. That's what kept me with her. I knew that loving, vulnerable person was in there, and I thought that by treating her well and taking care of her I could make all the difficulties she had experienced go away.

Leo came to live with us in the March of 1992. He was six months old and still very tiny, as he had been born three months premature. I couldn't believe that I had gone from being a single man in his mid-thirties to being, effectively, a father in such a short time. I resolved to be a good parent and got involved with the parenting chores, including bathing and nappy-changing, as soon as he arrived. Having children had not really entered my head since my previous girlfriend, Anne, had miscarried our baby in 1979. Here I was fitting into the role of a father, albeit not a biological one. Leo slept in the room adjoining Tina's bedroom and I took on more than my fair share of the getting up in the night rota, notwithstanding the fact that I was the one that was working full time and doing a fair amount of overtime once again too. Tina had taken some time off work in order to look after Leo; indeed this had been a condition of the residence order. I had my flat in London to maintain and a partner and child in Peterborough to take care of too. Tina was not keen for me to move in officially until we were married. I secretly found that attitude unbelievable as I reasoned to myself that she had moved Tom into her house without a second thought, but now that she had someone who really cared about her she was having doubts about me moving in.

In the end, Tina came around to my way of thinking. I rented out my flat in London through an agency in Streatham, and Tina's friend Sally drove me down to London in her small van to pack up my belongings and move them to Peterborough. . I was just concerned to earn sufficient from the rent to cover my mortgage. I did everything legally, and became an official co-tenant of Tina's local authority house. I remember looking at London as we drove through my home city for the past twenty-three years and wondering if I would ever live there again.

I found having a tiny child to look after an enjoyable challenge. Although I was working sixty hours a week or more, with over two hours travelling time to get into and home from work, I resolved to have one day every week that I would spend concentrating on Leo. I think Tina also saw this as an opportunity for her to get parenthood right, as she was beginning to open up and admit to me that she had not been the perfect mother for Hannah. Living with Tina was a life of extremes. Sometimes she could be the most loving and caring person I had ever met, and then she would change into a completely unreasonable and unpredictable person. I had no way of knowing which Tina I was going to wake up to in the morning, or come home to at night. Despite my uncertainty, I felt that I was in too deep to get out now. Plans went ahead for our wedding in August of 1992, and it was not going to be a quiet affair.

Tina's first marriage had been short-lived. She said that the wedding had taken place at the local register office and the reception had consisted of sandwiches and beer at her mother's house. My prospective mother-in-law had lived in Peterborough at the time of Tina's first wedding, and had apparently disgraced herself somewhat by being drunk at the wedding. I was determined that 'my Tina' was going to have her big day. Despite my misgivings about churches, a result of my over-zealous religious upbringing, I had bowed to Tina's wishes and agreed to get married in a Methodist church. The reception would take place in a country house hotel on the outskirts of Peterborough, the Haycock at Wansford. Tina had decided that she would rebuild relations with her estranged half-sister, and invite her and her husband to the wedding.

Part of the process of rebuilding Tina's relationship with her half-sister, Liz, involved Liz and her daughter Zoe coming to stay with us for a week. I had met Zoe before, earlier in the relationship, when Tina and I had gone to stay with her and her husband in Surrey. The week consisted of the three of them going shopping most days. Liz and her husband Harry owned several catering businesses in Bournemouth. It was quite apparent from the start that Liz looked down on me as I was a relatively lowly railway worker. I found her one of the most obnoxious and difficult people that I had ever had the misfortune to meet. She was dripping in gold jewellery, drove a flashy BMW and swore almost every second word. Liz chain-smoked expensive cigarettes and literally spent money like water. Tina confided in me that Harry had given Liz four hundred pounds spending money just to come to Peterborough for a few days. Tina obviously felt very inferior to her, and I tried to explain that having a lot of money didn't make anyone a better person. I told her that there was no way that I could afford to give her four hundred pounds to spend, but that didn't necessarily make me a bad person either. I felt almost intimidated by Liz, and was very glad that I was only at home for two days of her stay with us. I could see that Tina looked up to her, and I was worried that I was going to have to measure up to Harry in the financial stakes. There was no way that I could do that.

Tina told me that Liz had 'set her cap' at Harry a good few years earlier. Liz had Zoe, and also twin boys, Will and Tom, who apparently fought constantly and were a challenge to their mother. Harry was not the father of any of Liz's children. It was never made clear to me who the fathers were. I resolved that I would have as little to do with Liz as possible, and was very thankful that Liz and her family lived well over a hundred miles from us. My future mother-in-law also came down for a visit, to see her new great-grandson, and I saw a side of her that I hadn't seen when I went on the official visit to Manchester a few months previously. She was picky, morose, and only happy when she was the centre of attention.

Tina and I had an engagement party at a local pub a few weeks after we had announced our impending marriage. We invited a lot of our railway friends and many of Tina's friends and acquaintances from Peterborough came along too. I paid for everything, including a lot of the drinks. It was a very enjoyable evening and I felt proud to have Tina beside me for most of the evening. She looked particularly gorgeous that night. The day after the party we left Leo with one of Tina's friends for the day and went out to lunch at the home of one of our work colleagues. William and Peter were a rather flamboyant gay couple who both worked on the railway at the time. Tina got on particularly well with them and we had a great afternoon at their home. I remember eating the best lasagne I had ever tasted, drinking champagne and finishing off with sambuca. Tina was on great form for the whole weekend and I remember feeling very fortunate to have someone so vivacious and attractive in my life.

During the weeks leading up to our wedding there was a lot of preparation to do and much money to be spent. I had decided that I would splash quite a lot of my savings on the wedding. I reasoned to myself that I was only planning to do this once, and I wanted to see my new wife happy and radiant on her big day, so I would try to give her everything that I could. We decided to hire the bride's dress and the bridesmaid's dresses, and I bought a new suit, shirt, tie and shoes for the occasion. We were also both learning to drive. Tina passed her test first as she was the more experienced driver, and that meant that we now had the expense of keeping our old Ford Fiesta on the road. I was also still having to pay for taxis every day to and from the station to get to work in London, so household expenses were constantly rising. I told myself that this was all part of getting involved with someone and tried to get used to the constant demands on my wallet and cheque book.

Leo was a delightful little boy who was very easy to love. I was a little concerned at the amount of time that Tina had him propped in front of the television, but I would always spend time with him when I was at home. Tina didn't react very well to any suggestion that she could do something differently, and I was anxious to avoid confrontation, so she pretty much did what she wanted to. For my part, I pretty much did what she wanted me to do.

Chapter 20

More Demanding

I was beginning to have a few doubts about the whole wedding idea, in my heart of hearts. I was still uncomfortable with discussing this with anyone, because most of my close friends at work had taken to looking askance at me when I passed them, or when we worked together. I think a number of people were concerned about the turn my life was taking, but everyone was wary of saying anything to my face. I have been in that situation myself, when I have decided that the best thing to do to help someone is to say and do nothing!

Tina looked at me one night as we were watching television and said, 'I'm not marrying you unless you sort your teeth out.'

I have never been very good at going to the dentist. This all stems from an episode when I was a small child and went to the school dentist. The experience was so painful that I was not keen to repeat it, and I have consequently only visited the dentist when I have been in pain. I think the chemotherapy I had in the late 1970's also affected my teeth, and they have never been in the greatest condition. Tina was specifically referring to my front teeth, which were a mess, frankly, which was probably why I had tried to hide them with a moustache for many years, even after moustaches became deeply unfashionable! Tina did look after her teeth very well and went to a very good dentist in Peterborough city centre. She made an appointment for me and I went along with her in some fear and trepidation. The dentist was very professional and the surgery itself was the plushest I had ever seen. I had a feeling that making my teeth fit for my future wife was going to cost me a small fortune, and my feeling was proved to be correct when the dentist declared that the only way to sort out my front teeth was to have them all out and replace them with false teeth. I remember the thought flashing through my mind that it had not been part of my plan to have false teeth installed before I was forty years old, but I metaphorically gritted my teeth, while I still had some left, and signed up for the dentures. There was nothing, at that time, that I would not

236

do for Tina. I had to go back to the dentist two weeks later to have my front teeth removed and the new teeth put in place. I remember being in agony after the replacement of my front teeth and having to take a very rare day off work the following day while I recovered.

Meanwhile, I had failed my driving test at the first attempt, but thanks to the efforts of a very good driving instructor, Phil, I was able to pass at the second attempt. That gave me control of our Ford Fiesta, although Tina made it very clear that she had first claim on the car as she needed it to transport her and Leo around to various appointments. I was still paying for taxis to and from the station to get to work, despite paying for a car, and driving lessons and tests for two people. There was no doubt at all about who was in control of this relationship. It was not me.

A few weeks before the wedding we had an evening appointment with the minister of the Methodist church who was due to marry us. I had the day off work and had arranged to go to London to meet my old friend, John from Southend, who was to be best man at the wedding. He was working for a big financial services company in London

237

and had offered to take me out for a champagne lunch on his company credit card! I went out with John and was duly plied with champagne and a very good lunch in a restaurant in the City of London. I knew that I had to get home in good time for the appointment with the vicar, but unfortunately the champagne had other ideas, and I dozed off to sleep on the train back to Peterborough. The guard recognised me and woke me up when the train was approaching York, another hour and more further north from Peterborough. I phoned Tina from a phone box on York station, it being before the days of mobile phones. She was most unimpressed with the fact that I had dared to enjoy myself without her, but agreed to drive to the station and collect me. We would have to go straight from the station to the appointment with the Methodist minister. Luckily, there was a young girl, Vicky, who lived nearby and was happy to babysit Leo whenever we needed to go out together.

We arrived at the manse on time, although I was feeling somewhat hungover and Tina had let me know in no uncertain terms that I was in the dog house. My first impression on meeting the minister was that he was partial to a drop of hard liquor himself from time to time, and I immediately felt better. I had always been led to believe that Methodists didn't drink alcohol, but I have learned since that rules don't always apply to ministers and priests!

Our minister gave us a long talk about the importance of what we were embarking on, and impressed upon us the need to ensure that we were compatible in all areas of our relationship before we made the commitment of marrying each other. I sat there, feeling quite challenged, as I knew, in my heart of hearts, that we were not really compatible, and that I was heading for a major disaster.

When we got back in the car to drive home, I looked at Tina and asked her, 'Are you absolutely sure that you still want to marry me, because now is the time to say if you have any doubts?'

A brief shadow crossed her face, but she assured me that she was happy to continue our relationship and that we would work our differences out once we were married. I suppose I was so far in to the relationship that I was scared to go back, because I accepted what she said and we carried on. I am an eternal optimist and I thought that once we were married things would somehow miraculously improve. There was a small voice in my head most of the time telling me that this was not true, and that the whole relationship was destined to end in disaster, but I chose to ignore it completely. My life had changed for the better in some ways as a result of being involved with Tina. I no longer had time to think about my own problems because I spent most of my time helping Tina to deal with hers. Tina's problems became my problems. We were not even married yet, and she had completely taken over my life.

I had agreed to pay for the wedding and all the other sundry expenses associated with it. I had just switched off my common sense altogether when it came to the wedding and allowed Tina to have her own way on just about everything. I told myself that she had experienced a pretty rough life before she met me, so it was up to me to change that for her. She had decided that she wanted a Rolls-Royce to take her to the church, so that was what we had. Most of the people that were invited were her friends, although there were a number invited from work who knew both of us. Wedding invitations were chosen, ordered and sent out, after we had started with a long list of who we wanted to invite and then pared it down to eighty people for the whole day and another forty just for the evening. It was mostly my guests who were taken off the list. I'm sure there is nothing exceptional about this. Tradition dictates that a wedding is the bride's day, and I imagine that many men leave all the ideas and arrangements for their wedding to their bride-to-be.

The whole of Tina's extended family were to be invited, and that entailed re-building some of the relationships that Tina had allowed to fall by the wayside over the years. A cousin, Steve, suddenly appeared, living just a short distance from us, with his wife Jill and their two teenage children. Steve had his own roofing business and spent most evenings drinking in the local pub, *The Six Bells*. I formed the impression that Steve and Jill looked down on Tina a little, but they made us welcome when we went to their house for a drink and agreed to come to the wedding.

I think Tina felt that her life was taking a turn for the better and wanted to share it with all her family.

Liz and Harry, Zoe and Ken and their families had all accepted invitations to the wedding. Incredibly, given the fact that they were much wealthier than us, Liz told Tina that they expected to have their accommodation at the country house hotel paid for. I put my foot down at this point, which didn't go down at all well with Liz, who was used to getting her own way with her husband, who would do anything for a quiet life. I privately resolved not to be quite such a doormat as he was, although it was to be some time before I discovered the courage to go with that resolve!

Chapter 21

Changes at Work

During the run-up to our wedding, I had changed trains and was now working on the service that I would work for the rest of my front-line career on the railway. I was the Purser on the 08.00 Pullman from King's Cross to Glasgow. I had now returned to working three long days every week, although in practice that would usually be four shifts a week as I was finding the demands of running a house and keeping a partner and child quite strenuous and a drain on my resources. Tina had given up work for the time being to concentrate on taking care of Leo, and I had agreed to pay her a weekly amount so that she didn't have to ask me every time she needed some money.

The railway was starting to go through some changes. The first whispers about possible privatisation were starting to circulate and the organisation started to be managed much more like a business for the first time since I worked there.

As a Purser I was responsible for the profit and loss to a certain degree. I had regular and positive reviews with my boss who was starting to see me as someone who would eventually go into management or a support function. Tina always told how much everyone at work respected me. When I asked her what she meant, she said that she couldn't find anyone who would say a bad word about me. I secretly felt quite good about that, and it boosted my self-esteem at a time when I was not feeling good about myself in general.

One of the managers who tried to help me with my career during this period was Barry Lawrence. He was in charge of all the catering staff on the East Coast main line, and was either loved, or hated, by everyone. He was quite forceful and demanding, but I had the feeling that his heart was in the right place. The year that Tina and I got married, I decided to apply for a job in the Inter City training department. I felt that I had done all I could on the trains, and that the job was becoming a bit repetitive. The staff I was given were often not of a high quality, and I was frequently asked to make a silk purse out of a sow's ear.

The management would often put under-performing members of staff with me in the hope that I could 'do something with them'. I had been on an interviewing skills course as part of my Purser's training, but had never been asked to get involved in interviewing new recruits.

One day, I went to see one of the younger managers, Callum, to complain about the standard of staff that I was being provided with. I had a long conversation with him and managed to get him to allow me to come and sit in on some recruitment interviews a week or two later. What I saw and heard horrified me. The interview procedure had barely changed since I had had my interview for the railway in 1978, and it was now 1992. I remember one particular girl we interviewed that day. I wouldn't have given her a job in a fish and chip shop, let alone serving First Class passengers on my train who had paid hundreds of pounds for a ticket. I asked Callum where he got the interview questions from, and he said that he made them up as he went along. There was no change in this process for several more years. It was no wonder that the staff that were being employed were of such a poor standard – there was no proper person specification, or if there was, it was not being followed. Despite the railway having a massive personnel support function, I was to discover that many of the people who worked in that, and other support departments, were not exactly over-worked! I remember going home to Tina that night in a very pensive mood. I had started to realise how much work there was to be done if the world of the railway was to be changed for the better. I wondered what changes the rumoured upcoming privatisation would bring.

As part of the interview process for the job in training I had been asked to complete a psychometric test. I wasn't successful at the interview, and was asked to go and see Barry Lawrence for my interview feedback.

'Graham, we have to do something with you,' he said. 'Most of my managers are university graduates and yet your score in the psychometric test was comfortably better than all of theirs. I want you to consider a career change and go into management.'

I thought of the ridicule that I would get from my colleagues. The railway culture was very much them and us. Managers and staff didn't even drink in the same pubs in those days. I wasn't ready to be sent to Coventry by the people I had worked with for nearly fifteen years. Then he gave me a management vacancy list to look through. This list contained all the management vacancies in all departments throughout the whole of British Rail and was published every month. Mr. Lawrence drew my attention to a couple of jobs that he thought would be suitable for me. I noticed that the salaries were around £15,000 per year. With overtime and tips, I was earning over £20,000 in 1992.

'I can't go home to Tina and tell her that I'm taking a pay cut, Mr. Lawrence,' I said.

He advised me to think about it, and I did, for all of five minutes. Here I was, just about to get married and my boss wanted me to take a £5,000 a year pay cut! I knew what Tina would say, so I asked Mr. Lawrence to keep me in mind, and walked out of his office wondering if I had just put paid to ever taking the next step in my railway career.

247

The idea that I was more intelligent than some of the managers was not news to me. I had recently had a conversation with one of the junior managers that went like this.

'Graham, I've been meaning to ask you, why don't you sell more flapjacks on your train? You know there's a good profit margin on them.'

I had fixed the manager in question with what I hoped was an icy stare.

'The reason we don't sell more flapjacks is because we only get four a day. That's the standard order. We can't order any more, so when they are gone, they are gone.'

Two weeks later we started receiving a box of twenty-four flapjacks on our train every day. That was what the railway was like in those days. Full of managers who thought they knew everything, but many of them had come straight in from university or other businesses and had never taken the time to understand what went on at the sharp end of the business. As privatisation became a growing possibility, they felt under pressure to justify their existence, and put pressure on the front line teams to deliver better sales, so that they, the managers, looked good.

As privatisation began to be talked about more, we were expected to make money. As a Purser, I was responsible for the performance of my team. I had received a lot of training, but the support from management had never really been there. Once the train left London, we were very much on our own, and I had learned to cope with all sorts of challenges. Since we had moved to selling pre-prepared food, for example, we would frequently run out of food, and on other days we would have a lot of waste because the trains were quiet or we had some kind of operational problems that resulted in there being less passengers on board the trains. The new electric trains that we had looked wonderful, with their beautiful stainless steel kitchens, rotary toasters and built-in dishwashers, but none of this equipment had been designed to work while travelling at 125 miles per hour, and we would frequently be left to serve fifty or sixty breakfasts on our 08.00 business train to Scotland with equipment out of order. The general feeling among the staff was that if we were to be put under pressure to sell more food, we needed to have the equipment working properly and consistently in order for that to be achieved. To give Barry Lawrence his due, he was trying to bring all this to the attention of the powers-that-be at our head office in York, but it was a long battle.

One day we had the Director of Inter City travelling on the 08.00 with us. There couldn't have been more fuss if royalty had been travelling. I got into work even earlier than usual and went to check that sufficient food had been ordered. I bumped into a manager on the way to the stores. He was a decent guy who had worked on the trains, and he said he had already checked all my orders and everything was all right. The last thing I wanted was to run out of something with the Director on board. I knew him, he was a reasonable man, as most of the top brass on the railway tended to be. He and his wife had travelled with us on the Highland land cruises once or twice and I had met them then. They were very upper-class but I knew that he knew that I knew what I was doing! That morning, events conspired against us and the train didn't arrive on the platform at King's Cross until 07.50 for an 08.00 departure. We had to prepare the train in ten minutes, and the normal preparation time for a Pullman was at least one hour. To add to the problems, there was an army of managers, all desperate to be seen to be helping, getting under our feet. Barry Lawrence was running around in a creased shiny suit with an early brick-shaped mobile phone glued to the side of his head looking as if he would burst. The Director came up to the door of the train where I was desperately trying to get the supplies loaded on board, while the staff were running around trying to lay the tables.

'Morning, Graham,' he said. 'Anything I can do to help?'

I saw the expression on the faces of one or two of the junior managers who were hanging around trying to look important and helpful all at the same time, not an easy look to achieve. I could see that they were wondering how such an eminent person as The Director would know an insignificant body such as myself!

'No, thanks, sir,' I replied with what I hoped was a smile. 'We will get there eventually.'

A few moments after that the passengers boarded and we were away from King's Cross on time. After the guard had made his announcement I went on the public address system and made an announcement telling our passengers that there would be a short delay in the availability of the catering due to the fact that the train had arrived late on the platform, apologising and asking passengers to stay seated and await a further announcement.

Barry Lawrence came striding through the train, almost apoplectic.

'You can't say that with the Director on board!' he spluttered. Honestly, some railway managers really were like the Fat Controller from the Thomas the Tank Engine books. Barry's heart was in the right place, but he was very conscious that things should be seen to be done properly, especially with the boss of all bosses on board the train.

Of course, needless to say, we started serving breakfast in the restaurant car and things started going wrong. We had a starter trolley that one or two members of the team would take through the restaurant car. It contained breakfast cereal, fruit compote (a posh way of saying fruit salad) and glasses for fruit juice, which was contained in jugs. The Director of Inter City was sitting on the fourth table away from the kitchen, and requested fruit compote as his breakfast starter. This was the most popular starter by far at breakfast time and despite numerous requests I had not managed to get my order increased to more than six portions. We were serving an average of over forty breakfasts a day. One of my little jobs every morning was to increase my order so that we weren't refusing our customers their first choice of starter. However, because I had not personally checked my orders that morning, and had believed the very well-meaning manager who had said that all the orders were correct, the result was that the Director had to have an alternative starter for his breakfast, and, more to the point, so did ten or twelve paying customers further down the restaurant car. This may seem to be a very detailed explanation of a fairly insignificant event, but it was endemic of what was going on in the railway industry at the time. For years, we had been left to our own devices, and I knew that the service had been very inconsistent and, in some cases, non-existent, but I resented that I had managers climbing all over my train when I was one of the people who did know what I was doing. There was no follow-up to this day, no de-brief and I didn't hear another word from any of the managers about it. The Director got off the train at York and everything went back to being a normal day.

Chapter 22

Pre-Nuptials

I wasn't sure where I had more stress in my life at that point in time - home or work. Getting married is an expensive business, and I seemed to spend a lot of time signing cheques and withdrawing money from the bank. During my extended bachelorhood, I had salted quite a few thousand pounds away for a rainy day – it appeared that all my rainy days were approaching at once, despite the wedding being scheduled for August. It seemed that I was paying for everything that needed to be paid for – the only other event in my life that I could remember being so expensive was buying my flat in London in 1984.

One evening, as the date of the wedding approached, Tina asked me if I would do the seating plan for the wedding reception. I sat down at the kitchen table with the list of people who were attending, the seating plan and a pen. Somewhere between an hour and two hours later I had sorted out what I believed to be a fair seating plan. Tina had other ideas, and accused me of favouring my friends over hers. There were only a handful of my friends coming, most of the personal friends were Tina's, and there were a lot of railway colleagues coming. I had been to many of their weddings and celebrations over the years – indeed, in many ways, the railway had been my family since 1979.

In my opinion, a lot of Tina's friends were was I would refer to as 'ne'er do wells', and I wasn't looking forward to them all being in one place at a wedding in a respectable venue with a lot of alcohol being consumed. I didn't dare say that to Tina as she was very loyal to her friends, many of whom she had known since her school days. Eventually a compromise was reached. We would hand over the seating plan to Tina's friend Sally, and we would both stick to her decisions. This led to the interesting situation where a long-standing friend of mine from work and his wife were seated at the same table as a girl from work who was having an affair with him!

Wedding and bridesmaid's dresses were hired and I went out with Tina to buy a new suit, shirt, tie and shoes for the wedding. We had ordered our matching wedding rings and collected them from the jewellers. My long-standing and very good friend, John, was to be my best man. There had been a bit of a *fracas* over whether Tina's daughter Hannah was going to come to the wedding, but she had agreed to come in the end, even though she wasn't supposed to look after Leo, her son. It was all very unfortunate, and I could see a 'tug-of-love' situation developing. Tina had begun to think that she and I were going to have permanent custody of Leo, whereas I was of the opinion that we should only have him living with us until Hannah was emotionally and physically in the right place to have him with her. I tried to put all these difficulties to the back of my mind until after the wedding, a bit like someone who is expecting visitors desperately trying to tidy up an untidy house by stuffing things in cupboards and hoping that no-one would notice the half-open cupboard doors.

Tina had her hen night in Peterborough two weeks before the wedding. I remember being thankful that she had chosen to have her night out so long before the wedding so that all the dust would have settled before the happy day. I have no idea what went on at the hen night – she stayed at a friend's on the night in question and didn't appear home until the following afternoon, looking somewhat the worse for wear. We are talking about someone who could tuck away a bottle of vodka and then go out on the town. Of course, I was no slouch in the drinking department myself in those days. I had decided to have a quiet night in *The Engine House* at King's Cross for my stag night. I had been drinking in the pub after work for ten years and it was the nearest I had to a local. The landlord, Tony, put on a free buffet for us, and I sat with a dozen or so of my old railway friends, reminiscing about old times and piling away the pints of Webster's Yorkshire Bitter. My best friend John, who was also my best man, had come up from Southend, otherwise there were no 'non-railway' friends there. John had met my railway friends several times before, and enjoyed their company. We started quite early in the evening, and by 11pm I was ready to catch the last fast train back to Peterborough. There were to be no strip clubs or nightclubs for me on my stag night. I was turning into a respectable man now, with a ready-made family, and I had decided to go home to Tina and behave myself.

Just before I left the pub, Pete, one of the staff I had worked with occasionally on the charter trains over the years, came up to me.

'Frosty,' he said. 'There's a few of us thinking this, but no-one else will say it. Are you sure you're doing the right thing, marrying Tina? It's not too late you know, you can back out of it. You're a really great bloke and a lot of us think she's just using you...'

'I know what you're saying, Pete,' I replied, 'but my mind is made up and I'm going through with it. She needs me and I love her, that's all there is to it really.'

No more was said, and I went home to Tina, still relatively sober, probably eating a kebab on the 23.15 train back to Peterborough, thinking over what Pete had said and wondering what the outcome of my decision to marry Tina would be. I knew in my heart of hearts that I was not being true to myself, but there was a magnetism drawing me into this marriage and I had neither the wish nor the will to pull against it. I respected Pete for saying what a lot of people were thinking, but I was too far down the road with Tina to change anything now. I had talked myself into feeling that I was 'meant' to be with her, and what would happen to Leo if I was to abandon Tina now?

People say that moving house and getting divorced are two of the most stressful things that can happen in a person's life. I would add getting married to that list, because in the week or so leading up to the wedding I found myself wishing that it were all over so we could get back to living our normal life. I would imagine that getting married is stressful for most people, but when you are marrying someone whose daughter is barely on speaking terms with her, members of whose immediate family have not spoken to each other in years and there is also an eleven-month old baby to take care of, it certainly adds to the stress levels. Tina's mother had decided that she was not going to come to the wedding as her elder daughter Liz was going to be there, and they had not spoken in years. I found myself, not for the first time, thankful that none of my family would be there. I had written to my estranged parents telling them that I was getting married and received a very curt reply, just a few sentences from my father, telling me that it was obvious that I was still on the wrong path and that they were praying for me.

Tina was to be given away at the church by one of her nephews. She had not seen him for several years but they had spoken on the phone and arranged everything. Tina's sister Liz's two boys were apparently always at each other's throats, so it came as no surprise to me when, the day before the wedding, we received a phone call to say that they had both been arrested for fighting and wouldn't be coming to the wedding. We were left without anyone to give Tina away, until Liz's son-in-law, Ken, agreed to do it. I was quite relieved about that as he was quite a sensible guy and I knew he could be relied upon to turn up and at least not get drunk until after the event.

I had to continue to work in the run-up to the wedding. That helped me to keep my mind off the constant question that was going round my head. Was I doing the right thing? On the final day at work as a single man I was working with a strange crew – that is to say, I worked a train that I didn't usually work, with a crew that weren't used to me. I knew them all, but we didn't usually work together. Derek was a complete oddball of a man. He had been a Chief Steward when I had joined the railway in 1979, but had stepped down from that role and was now a steward. He would do the craziest things, such as stocking his sandwich cabinet in the buffet up with just one type of sandwich, and telling the passengers that was all he had. So, if you went to his buffet at 11am you could only buy a tuna sandwich, but if you went an hour later he would only have a cheese sandwich. In vain did I try to tell him that he couldn't do that, he just looked at me as if I was mad!

Chloe was another member of staff that I had known for a long time on that same trip. She decided that she was going to play a few tricks on me, as a bridegroom-to-be is fair game, and put jam on the public address microphone, which was shaped like a telephone receiver, so that when I picked up the handset to make an announcement I got strawberry jam in my ear. Derek also put a pair of kippers in my work bag that day, hoping that I wouldn't discover them until I returned to work after the wedding and honeymoon, but fortunately one of the other staff took pity on me and told me what he had done. I was, as you can imagine, extremely grateful. Imagine the stink after several weeks of festering!

My last day as a single man dawned. Tina had decided that she didn't want me to spend the night with her, as it was not 'the thing to do', so I was to stay with Georgie, Tina's elderly godmother, who lived a few streets away from us. I had been introduced to Georgie a few weeks before the wedding. I got the impression that Georgie didn't really approve of the way Tina had turned out, and looking back I can see why. Georgie had been widowed many years previously and lived in a house that was still decorated and furnished as if it were the early 1960s. It reminded me of my grandparents' house. Perhaps Georgie had not changed anything since her husband had died. She cooked me liver and onions for dinner and I sat down to chat with her. Georgie told me a few stories about Tina's mother, including the fact that she had been 'no better than she ought to be' when she was younger. She told me that Tina's mother had not really been a good wife to her husband, and gave me a searching look as if to say, 'Do you really want to marry the daughter of a woman like that?' I didn't take up the challenge.

I had arranged to meet some friends from work who were coming to the wedding from a distance and were staying in a hotel in Peterborough city centre. I excused myself and caught the bus into town for a quick couple of pints. I didn't want to think about what Georgie had said. I knew that it was unlikely that I would be happily married to Tina, but I thought I could make her happy. I figured that if she was happy, I would be happy. It's not a good foundation for marriage, to be at odds with the inner voice, but I carried on regardless.

I had two or three pints with my work friends and then got a taxi back to Georgie's house. I let myself in quietly and went to bed, tossing and turning in the uncomfortable single bed in Georgie's spare room. She had been very hospitable and kind, and I felt guilty for being a little ungrateful, but I did feel like a little boy staying at his grandmother's house that night, although I was a grown man of thirty-six years old. I probably slept for two or three hours, and Georgie kindly brought me a cup of tea in bed at 7.30am, and then cooked me a full English breakfast. I was not allowed near the nearby house where Tina was preparing for her big day. All I had to do was meet John and Kathy, my best man and his wife, make sure he had the rings, and get to the church on time. Friends were looking after Leo for the day and keeping him overnight. It was potentially the biggest day of my life. Here I was getting married for the first, and I believed, only time. I had been brought up in my family's church to believe that marriage was for life. Up until I was 17, I had never known anyone who was divorced, and that had made a big impression on me. It was one of my fundamental beliefs, despite the estrangement from my family. I felt that if I worked hard at being married to Tina everything would work out. I sat in the little armchair in Georgie's living room, deep in thought. It wasn't too late to escape. Georgie left the room and I was alone with my thoughts. No, I was going to make a go of this.

I finished my mug of tea, the third or fourth of the morning, and went outside for a cigarette. The sun was shining and it looked as if we were going to have good weather for our wedding. The cloud of doubt passed and I decided it was time to get ready for the big occasion. I had a bath, and dressed in my new suit, shirt, tie and shoes. Looking in the mirror, I thought I didn't look too bad in my finery. Everything fitted and I felt comfortable in it. I had arranged for someone to collect Georgie and take her to the church a little later. I shook her hand and thanked her for putting me up on my last night of freedom, and for the lovely breakfast. Friends of Tina's were driving our old Fiesta out to Wansford so we had transport home for the next day. We had booked a honeymoon in the Channel Islands, but were unable to leave until the Tuesday as we had a funeral to attend on the Monday. An old friend of Tina's mother's had passed away just a few days before the wedding and Tina felt that she should go to the funeral as her mother wasn't able to make it down from Manchester. Life as Tina's husband-to-be was not simple. I wondered how much things would change once we were married.

Chapter 23

The Big Day

I had arranged to meet John and Kathy, my best man and his wife, in Peterborough city centre. They were to drive me to the church for the wedding. When we met, we had an hour or so before we had to be at the church, so I suggested we go to a pub near the church for a beer. We turned up at the *Blue Boar,* just around the corner from the church, a pub that I had never been in before, and I ordered a drink for us all. After a few moments, I noticed that half of the railway catering staff from King's Cross were in the next bar. They had come up on an early train and decided to get stuck in to the beer before the wedding. I thought to myself that they were the least of my worries. Most of them could hold their drink and knew how to behave in polite company. It was good to see them, as I was quickly getting the feeling that I was in a movie and no longer had any control over what was going on in my life. I stayed with John and Kathy and waved across to my workmates. I knew that there were a good number of people at King's Cross who would always be there for me, no matter what.

Nick's wife, Karen, and her best friend, Tamsin, from my seemingly long-ago life in London arrived, and looked like fish out of water. There was no-one there that they would have had anything in common with; it was the same situation for them throughout the day. They had never met any of my work friends before, and I wondered, somewhat despairingly, what they would make of Tina's friends.

The time came for us to walk around the corner to the church. It was a modern building and not particularly church-like in appearance. I had been doubtful about getting married in a church – since leaving home at 17 I had steered clear of churches at every available opportunity, but Tina had wanted a church wedding so - here we were having one. I stood at the front of the church with John and waited for my prospective wife to arrive. I kept stealing looks behind me; most of the people in the church were looking as if they would rather be somewhere else. None of the people that I knew could be referred to as regular churchgoers and I doubted whether many of Tina's

268

friends regularly, if ever, darkened the doorstep of a place of worship.

Tina arrived and looked quite gorgeous in her wedding dress, on the arm of her niece's husband, Ken. Our minister, who looked as if he might have been a little the worse for drink the night before, conducted the ceremony, and at the end of the service, which consisted of some hymns and prayers, I realised that I was a married man. Oh, my word! Graham Frost, there is now a Mrs. Frost! What have you done? I don't think I have ever heard a less enthusiastic bunch of hymn-singers, myself included. That dis-empowered, in the midst of a movie feeling persisted. All in all, it was over very quickly and it was time to go outside for a few photographs, before the Rolls-Royce whisked us away to our country house hotel and the wedding reception. There were many more photographs there, and everything was videotaped too. The setting for the photographs was beautiful, beside the river at Wansford. We had chosen the venue because it was the most popular wedding reception location in the area. We were certainly not let down. The champagne reception was followed by a lovely buffet lunch where everyone was encouraged to eat as much as they possibly could. Tina and I walked into the room together and everyone stood and applauded. My first ever standing ovation! I had to chuckle to myself, looking over at the table where my old friend Jed and his wife were sitting with the girl he had been having an affair with for the past few months. The food and service were absolutely excellent, there was nothing to complain about, and even Liz, Tina's sister, who was used to the best of everything, looked impressed. Her husband, Harry, was a very quiet man who obviously gave her everything she wanted and let her do pretty much as she liked. I wondered if that was what I was going to turn into, now that I was married.

I was very pleased to be sitting next to my great friend John at the top table. He did a excellent job of the best man's speech, especially considering he hardly knew anyone in the room. I said a few words of thanks and Tina also got up and spoke, then the plates were cleared away and we cut the cake. The whole time, I felt as if I was acting a role out in someone else's life, and that this was not really happening to me. All the things that I had told myself that I would never do, had just happened. Get married, certainly in a church, marry someone that I wasn't absolutely sure of, give up my independence – here they were, all gone in a day!

Another forty guests arrived for the evening party and everyone else continued drinking and making merry, just like happens at most weddings. I still felt as if I was having an out-of-body experience when the disco started up. Tina and I had requested Van Morrison's 'Have I Told You Lately...?' for our first dance, but the hotel had not passed our request on to the DJ. I couldn't think off the top of my head what substitute song to ask for, in the end I settled for 'When A Man Loves A Woman' by Percy Sledge. It wasn't that it was one of my favourite songs, it was just the first suitable record that came to mind. I was disappointed that we had not had our original song as we both genuinely liked it and it meant something to us as a couple. Underneath all my doubts I was very fond of Tina. I wanted all the partying to be over so that we could be together and try to make things work as a married couple.

We had a few dances together and then went around and talked to everyone. My friends Karen and Tamsin from my London days had left early, possibly feeling uncomfortable, because they didn't know anyone apart from me. They were lovely people and great friends, but they came from very middle-class backgrounds and didn't really have anything in common with railway people and the working and non-working people of Peterborough who made up most of the guests. I remember reflecting on what a mixed bunch of people I had made friends with during my nearly twenty years in the real world after leaving my religious upbringing behind. I wondered if I would ever see Nick, Karen, Tamsin and my other friends from my London days again.

If Tina and I had ever had any ideas of quietly slipping off together they were put paid to by Tina's sister Liz and her family. We ended our evening at about 4am, having sat for at least two hours drinking large brandies and black coffees with Liz, Harry, Zoe, and Ken. They certainly knew how to drink, and I remember wending my way up to bed after 4am on rather unsteady legs. Tina and I became one of the many couples who, I'm sure, on their wedding night, tumble into bed together, exchange a few pleasantries and fall asleep. As I have said before, the physical side of our relationship was never great for either of us, and our wedding night was no exception.

It seemed like just two hours later when the alarm bell rang and it was time to get up, shower and dress, and head down to breakfast where we had arranged to meet a number of our guests who had stayed at the hotel overnight. I remember looking at Tina over the breakfast table and realising that here I was, having breakfast with my wife. What had I done? All things considered, she was very attractive and had thoroughly enjoyed her wedding day. There was still a lot to sort out between us, but I was hopeful that the week we were about to spend in Guernsey together would cement our relationship and that I would come back from honeymoon feeling more positive about life with my new wife and new life.

Chapter 24

After The Lord Mayor's Show

As soon as we had finished our breakfast, it was time to say good-bye to our friends and guests who were all driving home after the weekend of celebrations. I was not sorry to say good-bye to Liz, my new sister-in-law. I knew she looked down on me because I wasn't wealthy like her husband. There were many good friends from work who had stayed over, and I thanked them all for coming and for the lovely presents that we had received. We had done very well for a couple who already had everything that we really needed. Next, it was time to pack as many of the presents as we could into our little Ford Fiesta, and I drove Tina home. I had to make a second trip back to *The Haycock* to collect a second load of presents, and Tina's hired wedding dress. I remember reflecting that there I was, driving along in an old rust bucket of a car, having just spent goodness knows how much on a wedding. Where had my priorities gone? What was happening to my life? Where had all the money gone that I had been saving for a rainy day?

The day after the wedding was a complete anti-climax. We were at home, just the two of us, Leo was back with us, and it was just a normal day. We had planned to go away on honeymoon on the Monday, but we had a funeral to attend, which is one way of being brought down to earth after a fairytale wedding day. I remember sitting watching television with Tina that Sunday evening, and thinking that nothing had really changed. Here we were, two people who had come across each other and thought that we could make a life together. There was nothing else for it, I was going to have to work very hard at the marriage, because I knew in my heart of hearts even then that I was the one that was going to be doing most of the work.

I had met Tina's mother's old friend Doreen a few times. She had been confined to a wheelchair for the last few years of her life, and Tina had taken me to see her in her little flat a couple of times. Tina was very emotional at her funeral and I had to spend a lot of time comforting her. I think because I had walked away from my family at an

275

early age I had closed off all the normal family emotions –
I knew, for example, that my grandparents must have
passed away by the mid-1980's, but I had banished all
thoughts of them from my mind a long time before.
Perhaps that was why I was unable to feel any emotion at
Doreen's funeral. We attended a small wake for her and
then went home to prepare for our departure to Guernsey
the next morning.

We had booked Guernsey because Leo was coming with
us. He was due to have his first birthday while we were
away, and we had been advised not to take him too far
from home as he was still very small for his age. The travel
agency in Peterborough had recommended the Channel
Islands, which neither Tina or I had visited before, and we
had chosen a hotel that catered for honeymoon couples and
babies. I had never had a holiday so close to home before –
I was more used to the Greek islands, and Tina's holidays
had usually been trips to Spain and the Balearic Islands.

On the Tuesday after we were married, we drove to
Stansted Airport in our old Ford Fiesta to start our
honeymoon. We were booked to fly British Airways to

Guernsey. I was surprised to see that the aircraft was a small 24-seater with propellers. Tina was quite worried as she had never flown in such a small plane before. Leo was with us, and it was his first flight, although he was still at the stage of his young life where he spent much of the time asleep. I will always remember that flight because it was so short. We took off, the elderly stewardess served us and the other ten or twelve passengers tea and a scone, and by the time we had finished the snack, the plane was landing. I had arranged to collect a hire car at the airport and we were soon on our way to the hotel in St Peter's Port. We had seen pictures of the hotel in the brochure at the travel agents' but we were not prepared for how old-fashioned it was. The room was very antiquated and quite basic. I almost expected to see a 'po' under the bed, but thankfully there was an en suite bathroom. I can only imagine what Tina would have said if she had had to go down the corridor for the bathroom during the night! I had been expecting something a little more modern for what we had paid, but I have always been the sort to try and make the best of a bad job, so decided to get on and enjoy our honeymoon.

277

It's not easy, taking your almost one-year old step-grandson on honeymoon. Having Leo with us meant that we could not really leave the hotel after dinner in the evenings, so we had to avail ourselves of the entertainment that was to be found in the hotel, which consisted of playing bingo, and listening to some truly awful music. It was as if someone had transported a working men's club from the North of England into the Channel Islands, on top of a basic boarding house. I am not a snob, but Tina was fast becoming one, and she was quite vocal in her protests. Every time she wanted to dry her hair in our hotel room she had to find 10p and put it into a meter. Of course, we had Leo in a cot within our room too, so it was a slightly uncomfortable situation at night. Add to all of this the fact that it rained for most of the week, and you will begin to understand that our lives as Mr and Mrs Frost got off to an inauspicious start. Tina was a sun-worshipper, and loved nothing more than relaxing in the sun all day. With no sun to relax in, the week became a treadmill of sightseeing, visiting jewellery shops and looking askance at each other. The word 'divorce' was mentioned in the first half of the week, and not by me. It is possible to drive around

Guernsey in less than a day, and we did that several times! On the Thursday, the sun shone, and we were able to spend the day on a beach, but apart from that our honeymoon was an endless round of wondering what to do next to fill the time. The little voice in my head was telling me that I had made my bed, and would probably have to lay in it for a good while yet.

I am sure that there are many couples who struggle with their relationship when they are first married. I had known in my heart of hearts that being married to Tina was not going to be easy. After all, being her boyfriend for the best part of a year had hardly been a bed of roses. I tried very hard to do all the right things, and occasionally Tina would respond in a positive way, but it was an uphill struggle. I resolved to tell her that I loved her every day, and I did so, but my affirmations of love were often greeted with the response, 'I don't know why....' or completely ignored. I began to realise that Tina had married me for security and to have someone to help bring Leo up, and that was the story. I decided to be as good a provider and husband as I could and to see if that wouldn't turn things around. All I wanted was someone who would be happy to see me when I walked through the door and would enjoy spending time with me.

Chapter 25

Reality

We returned from Guernsey late in August 1992 and found the bill from the hotel for the wedding on the doormat when we arrived home. We had paid for some of it upfront but the bar bill for the day was over £600. It was another large cheque to be written out. Then I took the hired wedding and bridesmaid's dresses back to the store. There was a small cigarette burn in one of the dresses, so I lost the deposit on that. I realised that I had almost exhausted my life savings. I had always been very good with money and had never borrowed a penny, apart from my mortgage. There I was, married to someone who appeared to think that money grew on trees. I slowly came to the realisation that things were going to have to change if we were to have a successful marriage.

I went back to work the day after we returned from our honeymoon. I realised that I was going to have to put in a fair amount of overtime if I was going to replenish the coffers that had been left dangerously depleted by the wedding and honeymoon. While we were away Tina had seen a rather expensive ring that she obviously wanted. I had secretly told myself that I was going to buy it for her as a Christmas present, and Christmas was only a few months away. I set out my stall at work. I would work as much overtime as they would give me, but I would take at least one day off every week. I also contacted my old bosses at the charter trains office and told them that I was available on Saturdays whenever they wanted me. When Tina raised objections I told her that she could either have me at home two or three days a week or she could have something approaching the lifestyle she obviously craved, but she couldn't have both.

Before long I was working more hours than I had ever worked before, and had the additional strain of over two hours travelling to get to and from work. My alcohol consumption dropped significantly. I would sometimes drink a can of beer when I got home from work, but the after work trips to the pub had stopped completely. With an eighty-mile journey home after fourteen-hour shifts, the last thing I wanted was to waste time in the pub!

On my days off, Tina encouraged me to spend time with Leo. We had a long discussion about what we were going to bring him up to call us. Tina wanted him to call us Mummy and Daddy, but I strongly objected to that. I said that we were not his Mummy and Daddy, and that the whole idea of him living with us was only a short term solution. This was one of the very few things that I was adamant about, and we ended up bringing Leo up to call us Nanny and Papa. I was not keen to be referred to as 'Granddad' at thirty-six years of age. Tina, at approaching thirty-nine was even less keen on being called Nanny, until I explained that it sounded better than Grandma.

Deep down, I knew that Tina saw looking after Leo as an opportunity to right a few wrongs. She had not been a perfect mother to her daughter, Hannah, and while she would never talk about this at length or in depth, I knew that she would have done a lot of things differently if she had her time over again. I would not like readers to labour under the misapprehension that Tina and I fought all the time. We did have some very tender moments together, and I genuinely loved her, but there were some times when I knew that I had probably taken on the biggest challenge of my life.

We hadn't been married for very long when Hannah started being allowed to have Leo with her on a Saturday. Tina was not keen, but the authorities, who were still very much involved in Leo's life, had decided that she was in a good enough place to be able to look after her son for a few hours at a time. I had still not managed to build any sort of a relationship with Hannah. I had no experience of mixed-up teenagers and was rather wary of her. For her part, I don't think she knew what to make of me at all. I was very different to her mother's usual partners, from what I understood. Hannah had no contact with her father at that point and probably felt completely alienated from reality but I was not to begin to understand her for a few more years yet.

Leo was beginning to be a joy to be with. I started spending one day a week with him, just the two of us. I would take him for a drive in the car and then get out and walk for a while, somewhere in the countryside around Peterborough, often with him sitting on my shoulders. Having children had never really been part of the plan for me. I had always felt that it was such a responsibility, and I had a hard enough time keeping myself on the straight and narrow without worrying about another small person who would look at me and want to be like me. But I enjoyed Leo's company. One particularly happy day I had taken him to a farm a few miles out into the country and we had looked at the sheep, pigs, goats and cows. I decided to take him for a long walk on my shoulders, and after about twenty minutes I realised that I was talking to a small boy who had fallen asleep on my shoulders. I managed to get him down without dropping him and carried him back to the car, which was at least a mile away Leo loved to ride on my shoulders and I rarely took the pushchair when we went on our little trips. It meant a lot to me that he felt safe enough with me to fall asleep on my shoulders as we walked along in the countryside.

Another particularly happy moment from our times together was shortly after Leo had learned to walk. Tina brought him down to London one Sunday to meet me off the train I had worked. He saw me in the distance and was literally jumping up and down with excitement. They were lovely moments and I will always treasure them. I knew that he was only with us for a short time, until Hannah was ready to have him to live with her, so I was determined to make the most of him.

Looking back on those early months of marriage, I think Tina and I were both trying to play the role of what we thought a good husband or wife should be. I was very much focused on being the provider, and Tina, who unlike me had not had great role models in her own childhood, was trying to be what I wanted her to be. Neither of us were very good at communicating what it was that we really wanted from the other.

Chapter 26

Christmas

From what I could understand, Tina and Hannah had almost always managed to bury the hatchet for long enough to spend Christmas Day together. They had the sort of mother/daughter relationship where there would be hugs and kisses and protestations of undying love, followed very closely, after alcohol had been consumed, by blazing rows, swearing and sometimes physical violence towards each other. I had never witnessed this sort of behaviour before, but Tina's friends had told me, in confidence, that I was now a part of this sort of relationship.

For our first Christmas together as a married couple, with Leo, Tina decided to invite Hannah to spend the day with us. She arrived on Christmas Eve, and I have to say that she scrubbed up well. Most of the times that I had seen her before, she seemed to be making a huge effort to be as untidy and challenging as possible, but it seemed that she was really making an effort on Christmas Eve 1992. Tina and I had been to the supermarket and spent an absolute fortune on food and drink, and the cupboards and fridge were groaning under the weight of the food and booze. I had never met anyone who consumed so conspicuously over Christmas, but I was trying to enter into the spirit of the time of year. The ring that Tina had wanted when we were on honeymoon in Guernsey had been purchased and wrapped, the house had been decorated with a large Christmas tree and many other decorations and there were many Christmas cards on display. The Frosts were a popular family and we wanted everyone to know it!

On Christmas morning I got up early and went down to prepare breakfast in bed for Tina and Hannah. We had buck's fizz and smoked salmon with scrambled egg on wholemeal toast for breakfast that Christmas morning. If I say so myself, I do make a mean scrambled egg, and I was feeling very pleased with myself as I placed Tina's tray in front of her, with her Christmas present prominently displayed. She ignored the food and tore off the packaging on her present, and opened the ring box.

'That's the wrong one,' she pouted, glaring at me.

'Mother...' interjected Hannah. 'Don't be so ungrateful.'

'Ungrateful?' said Tina. 'You knew which ring I wanted, can't you ever do anything properly?'

I took my breakfast tray back downstairs and ate my breakfast alone, in silence. The buck's fizz tasted bitter in my mouth now, but I drank it down and ate my breakfast. So that was what it had come to. I thought back to my days living alone in London and wondered what had possessed me to think that I would be happy living with someone who so obviously only wanted me for my money and wasn't really interested in me as a person at all. I finished the bottle of champagne off for good measure. Fine, if that was what she wanted, I could be uncaring and inconsiderate too. I washed up and went upstairs to collect the rest of the dishes. Walking into the bedroom, Tina and Hannah were cuddled up on the bed together like a real mother and daughter on Christmas Day. Well, that was something, I suppose, at least they were having a good day. Leo was still asleep in his cot, so I decided to go downstairs and start preparing lunch. I was marginally the better cook than Tina, well, slightly more than marginally if the truth be told, and I enjoy cooking, so rather than sit and mope, I got everything ready for lunch.

After a while I could hear baths running and soon Tina and Hannah appeared with Leo, who was looking for his breakfast. There was a massive box in the middle of the living room floor, which contained his present from us, a large Wendy House, which was to be set up in the garden. I helped him to unwrap it while Tina and Hannah sorted him out some food and drink. He spent most of the rest of the day climbing happily in and out of the large box that the Wendy House had come in, totally ignoring the contents of the box. At sixteen months old Leo was a happy little boy and I was very thankful to have him in my life. I was very disappointed that I seemed to have married such a self-centred and unappreciative woman, but I was enjoying being a substitute father for Leo so decided to concentrate on the positives. Christmas Day went along without any further dramas. Even Tina and Hannah got along well and anyone looking through the window into our lives that day would have seen what they would have imagined was a perfectly normal family enjoying Christmas together.

Boxing Day was a different story. Tina had told me that she was inviting 'a few friends' round for a drink and a bite to eat in the afternoon. I hadn't been too keen on the idea, but the invitations had gone out before Tina had told me, so there was little point in protesting. Our guests started arriving at about two in the afternoon and soon there were twenty or so of them in the house, drinking our beer and wine, and eating our food. I knew some of them slightly, some of them quite well, but they all had one thing in common. They arrived empty-handed and left as soon as we ran out of drink. Over a hundred pounds worth of beer, wine and spirits gone in an afternoon. I had never experienced anything like it! If I ever went to someone's house for a party, I always took a drink with me, and usually something that people would want to drink. When I mentioned to Tina that we had practically run out of booze, with New Year's Eve still to come, she gave me a strange look and told me that the shops would be open the next day and we could stock up again. I think I made some mention of the fact that she was labouring under the misapprehension that she had married a millionaire, and that I thought a mystery visitor had cut down the money tree in the garden a few weeks ago, but by this time I knew better than to put up too much of a fight, so resigned myself to another trip to the supermarket to stock up again the next day.

Christmas Day and Boxing Day are the only two days of the year that the railway is completely closed, so I was almost looking forward to going back to work on the day after Boxing Day. No-one particularly enjoyed working over the Christmas holiday period as the trains are usually full of people who don't want to be there. Millions of people in the UK spend Christmas with relatives out of a sense of duty, and are miserable on the way there, and often hung over and even more miserable on the way home. The railway staff often have to bear the brunt of this misery, and woe betide a member of staff who is unable to satisfy the demands of these once-a-year travellers, who expect to have every need met by a skeleton crew of staff who were usually completely under-resourced and demotivated. The difference between the railway of Monday-Friday business services and weekend trains is massive. There are virtually no business travellers at weekends so the railway has traditionally believed that leisure travellers do not need service, they just need to get from A to B. I was more and more beginning to wonder, by 1992, if I would not be of more use to the railway family by going to work behind the scenes to improve the lot of the staff and customers.

Chapter 27

'Tina'isms'

Married life went on from one day to the next, one week to the next, and one month to the next. Occasionally, Tina would do something really lovely, like having a meal ready for me when I returned from a day's work, and being really loving towards me, but I could count the times that happened during our time together on the fingers of one hand. Her mother had always told her to 'treat them mean and keep them keen' and I really believe that Tina thought that it truly was the way to keep a man. I saw her brother-in-law Harry and realised that I was going to turn into a door mat like him if I wasn't careful. Work became a respite for me, and I accepted every day's overtime that I was offered, even when I knew it meant working crazy hours. There was one day a week that was sacrosanct, and that was the day that I always spent playing with Leo.

I got home from work one day to find Tina playing with a new mobile phone.

'Look at this', she said, 'isn't it brilliant?'

I gave her a quizzical look. 'What do you want one of those for?' I asked.

'So I can talk to my friends' she said.

'I would have thought you could have talked to your friends on the normal phone. Besides, how many of your friends have got mobile phones?'

'Well, none, but I can talk to them on their house phones on it'.

'But you have a cordless phone that even works in the garden, I would have thought that was enough'.

I got a really good deal from that new mobile phone shop in Millfield'.

'OK, well, you've got it now, haven't you, but be careful with it. I've heard they can be really expensive. The only people I knew at this point who had mobile phones were senior managers on the railway. Soon, she would be sitting in the garden phoning people on their landlines and saying loudly, so that all the neighbours could hear, 'I'm on my mobile.'

A few weeks later, when the first bill for her mobile phone came in things came to a head. I got home from work one night to face it.

'I've got a bit of a problem, love.'

'What's that?'

'Well, my mobile phone bill's come and it's eighty quid.'

'What's that got to do with me?'

'Well, I was hoping you might help me out with it. You know I'm not working at the moment.'

'Have you heard the expression 'no hope or Bob Hope'?'

'That's not very nice.'

Now, I was paying all the household bills, rent and giving Tina a tidy sum every month to cover her expenses and Leo's clothes, in addition to paying for all the groceries, but she somehow expected me to cover her for unnecessary luxuries as well.

Tina had assumed responsibility for the weekly shop, but I was concerned that she was going to the supermarket and coming home with a car-load of shopping, only for one of us to have to pop to the local convenience store on a regular basis during the week. She was spending a hundred pounds a week at the supermarket and then heaven knows how much was being spent on bits and pieces during the week. I sat her down one evening.

'Tina, love, I think I'm going to have to start doing the weekly shopping'

'Why's that?'

'Well, you seem to be spending an awful lot of money when you go to the supermarket and then we are having to go shopping for bits and pieces during the week, it's

297

costing well over a hundred quid a week and we can't afford it'

'Well, you're earning good money, aren't you?'

'Not good enough money to be wasting it unnecessarily'

'Are you saying I waste money?'

'Not exactly, just that you could be a bit more careful with it – we need to be able to afford a holiday this year, and we won't be able to the way things are going'

'Well, if you want to start doing the shopping, that's fine with me. You can take Leo with you on your day off and that will give me some time to myself. I bet you'll forget half the stuff'. .

I started doing the weekly shop for seventy pounds and there were hardly any additional trips to the corner shop. I did find myself accused of acting as if there was a war on, but I stuck to my guns. There was always plenty of decent quality food in the house and generally alcohol available too!

Six months into 1993, Tina had a phone call from work. A part time job, three afternoons a week, had come up at King's Cross station, and she was asked if she was interested in it. She had found someone who could look after Leo for the two afternoons that I wouldn't be available, and asked me what I thought of the idea. I was flattered to be asked, because Tina usually went ahead and did things without talking them through, and then came to me to sort things out when they went wrong. I was supportive of her in this idea, as I thought it would give her some independence again and being in work would help when the inevitable happened, and Leo went back to live with his mother, Hannah. Tina did end up taking the job, and we had a massive argument about whether I was going to continue to pay her 'allowance' every week once she was back at work. Tina said that she would be no better off working than she was at home if I stopped paying her the weekly sum. In the end, we compromised. I said that I would pay the child care costs incurred by her returning to work, which, in fact, was less than the amount that I was paying her weekly anyway. The young lady who looked after Leo when Tina went back to work was the daughter of a colleague of mine at work, a nice young woman called Christine. Tina, who also knew Christine's mother, took it upon herself to start treating this young woman like a servant, and I had to go around to her house several times to smooth over the difficult situations that Tina had created.

The old Ford Fiesta had died, and I had bought an early diesel Ford Escort from Christine's partner. He had fitted it with wide wheels for some reason, and I thought it looked quite sporty, but in truth it was like driving a tractor. It was only my car in name, as Tina used it more than I did.

I would not want to leave you with the impression that my wife was a talentless, negative person. Tina had a great flair for interior design, and the inside of the house was always immaculate and tasteful. This had not necessarily been the case when I first came into her life, but since we were married, the re-designs and shifting of furniture became almost constant. I came from a family where we had only ever had anything new when something wore out, and now I was expected to buy two new sofas in a year! I often got home from work to find that something I had left on the side in the kitchen had been 'tidied away', often into the bin. The lounge was re-organised almost weekly, and I never knew where anything was. The house was always very clean, however. I would sometimes dust and vacuum while Tina was at work, but my cleaning was never up to her exacting standards. I enjoy ironing, but after struggling to iron a white pleated skirt to Tina's high standards one day I told her that she could do her own ironing and I would do mine.

I think you may be able to see a picture of unparalleled domestic bliss emerging here. I found myself socialising with other colleagues at work who had difficult marriages. I had completely lost touch with all my London friends and hardly ever saw my friends John and Kathy from Essex, who I had known for many years. I didn't want anyone to know how dissatisfied I was with my lot in life, so I just associated with other people who were as unhappy as me. The thought of spending the rest of my life in that relationship was very difficult. I had married in haste, and now I would repent at leisure. Despite my lack of religious conviction, I did believe that marriage should be worked at, and was reluctant to give up on the relationship with Tina. She had mentioned that it might be a good idea for me to sell my flat in London and buy her house outright, but I was determined to hang on to my lifeline.

Chapter 28

Another Holiday

Less than a year after our wedding, we were off on holiday again. I was determined that we were going to have a holiday abroad every year, and had managed to salt away enough money over the year to fly off to Rhodes for a fortnight, despite mobile phone bills and Tina's general profligacy with money To give Tina her due, she did always say that I was a great provider. I had been to Rhodes before, and we booked into a big family style hotel in Lindos. Leo was with us, of course, he was just short of his second birthday. He had started to toddle around, but still spent a lot of time asleep. Tina told me that she was going to tell anyone we met on holiday that we were his Mum and Dad, as that was easier than having to explain the truth.

'I'm sorry, Tina' I said, 'There is no way that I am agreeing to that. Why can't we just tell people the truth? I'm not ashamed of it!'

'I just think it would be easier' she replied. 'I don't want a whole load of strangers knowing my business'.

In the end, we compromised – we wouldn't tell anyone, we would leave them to ask. It wasn't as if I was going to walk around wearing a t-shirt bearing the legend 'I'm this child's step-grandad and I'm only 37'. Tina was getting uncomfortably close to her 40th birthday and was not particularly looking forward to entering the fifth decade of her life.

We flew to Rhodes from Luton Airport, which was easier to drive to from Peterborough, so I drove the car from Peterborough to Luton Airport and used the airport car park.. We also had Leo's push chair and all the other necessities for taking a small child on holiday for two weeks. We were fortunate to have booked into a great hotel and the food and accommodation were more than acceptable. Being part of a couple was unusual for me, but being part of a couple with a child was a completely different experience. As I was still a non-swimmer, Tina taught Leo to swim and we managed to get through the holiday without too many cross words. We met two or three other couples who had small children and got on quite well with them, which was a great blessing, as I hadn't much been looking forward to spending two whole uninterrupted weeks with Tina. That is a terrible admission to make after less than a year of marriage, but it was true nonetheless. We got on particularly well with Gary and Sue, a couple from Shropshire who had two young daughters. Sue was very attractive and I had to make sure my eyes didn't wander in her direction too often when we were sitting around the pool chatting. Tina had gained weight since we had been married and I knew she was conscious of that. The last thing I wanted was to upset her by looking at other women when she was around.

There was one particular guy on the fringes of our little group on that holiday. He was there holidaying with his wife, and seemed to be in awe of her. It was almost as if he had to have his wife's permission to breathe. We sat on the same table with them at dinner one night, and he was politeness personified, when he could get a word in edgeways, as his wife was one of those people who always talk about themselves and what they have got. Tina quite liked her, but I was dubious. The next day, the guy came over to the poolside bar when Gary and I were having a mid-afternoon pint and a chat there, and proceeded to tell us all about his life, with the most uses of the 'f' word that I have ever heard in my life, and I have been in prison and worked for the railway! I have literally never seen such a transformation in someone when they are apart from their wife. I made a mental note never to turn out like that!

Tina was one of those people who could happily sit by a pool for an entire two week holiday, but I get itchy feet after a day or two of that, and like to explore wherever I am staying. Gary and Sue hired a car for a day or two, so I suggested to Tina that we should do so too and go off for a drive around Rhodes. She agreed, and I hired a tiny Daewoo car for two days. It was the first time I had driven on the right hand side of the road, and Greek drivers are not, perhaps, as disciplined as their British counterparts, so it was with some trepidation that I set off to drive to the other side of Rhodes. We arrived safely, however, and spent a very enjoyable day with Gary and Sue, and their children, on the beach.

Tina had tried to tempt Sue into a shopping trip, but thankfully Sue appeared not to enjoy shopping as much as Tina did, so I had been spared the wallet-emptying effects of one of Tina's shopping sprees! Tina wanted to drive back to Lindos, but I was dubious about letting her drive there as she did not have her driving licence with her and I had hired the car and put myself down as the named driver. That caused a massive argument in the car on the way back and was the first bad moment of the holiday. We were in the second week by that time and I was beginning to look forward to going back to normality. I kept the car for a second day and went off for a drive on my own into the mountainous area of Rhodes at the other end of the island. I needed to be alone for a day. I spent the day ruminating over the position I had got myself into with Tina. I knew it was not going to be a successful marriage, but I felt that I was in the middle of a long tunnel and I had lost sight of both ends. Driving along in the tiny car I lost focus on where I was going and ended up on a mountain track that was unpaved and almost vertical. Luckily, I managed to turn the car around before I got stuck completely, and I headed back to the hotel and my loving wife!

We had taken a camcorder on holiday and Tina took it everywhere we went. In the evenings there was a karaoke competition at a neighbouring hotel, and we started going there after dinner. Tina was a great singer and won the contest twice. Eventually, she managed to persuade me to take part, and I went on stage and selected my song. For some reason, I thought John Lennon's *Imagine* would be an easy song to sing, and I chose it. About two lines into the song I realised that it was a very difficult song, but I tried gamely to finish it. It was one of the most embarrassing moments of my life, and Tina had recorded it on the camcorder for posterity.

Leo thoroughly enjoyed his first proper holiday abroad and was royally spoiled by Gary and Sue's two little girls. He was almost two years old and into everything, although he still spent a lot of time sleeping. Leo had been responsible for a huge change in my lifestyle. I still smoked, as did Tina, but I had cut down tremendously on the amount of alcohol I drank, as I didn't want Leo to grow up in a house where there was a lot of drinking. I had realised that I needed to be a positive role model for him, although it was to be a long time before I gave up smoking.

When we arrived back at Luton Airport after our holiday in Rhodes, Tina got her revenge on me for not letting her drive the hire car in Lindos. She drove home from Luton Airport triumphantly, having left me to pay the £45 cost of parking our car at the airport for two weeks. I wouldn't want anyone to think that there was no affection between Tina and me. We did have our moments of affection, but they were now few and far between. Most of the time, it seemed as if we were scoring points off each other.

Chapter 29

Changing Lifestyle

Moving to Peterborough and marrying Tina had totally changed my life. I had gone from being an independent man with a number of friends to focusing on Tina and Leo to the almost total exclusion of everyone else. My social habits had changed. I no longer smoked marijuana because the railway had introduced a Drugs and Alcohol Policy that applied to all staff. If you were caught with any trace of illegal drugs in your system at any time, you would be instantly dismissed. Similarly, the level of alcohol that staff were allowed to have in their bloodstream was now fixed at about a quarter of the legal limit for driving a car. All the staff had been briefed on the new rules, and we were well aware of the severity of the punishments. I was approaching my late thirties and had fifteen years service under my belt. The railway had been very good to me, and I wanted that to continue. I had no idea what I would do if I lost my job, so I complied willingly with the new rules. I was also driving a fair amount now, so had to watch my alcohol consumption for that reason too. When I finished work I would be straight on the first train home to Peterborough and rarely if ever went for a drink at King's Cross any more.

I had also taken up gardening. Tina's house had quite a large garden, which was rather overgrown when I first met her. I had hacked all the vegetation back and created a pleasant area for us to sit in during the summer. I also hired a chainsaw and trimmed back the trees and bushes. Decorating the house was outside my comfort zone, so when Tina suggested one day that the whole ground floor of the house needed re-modelling I asked her if she had anyone in mind who might be able to do that for us. Several months, thousands of pounds and much overtime on my behalf later we had a new ground floor for the house. While most of the work was being done, Tina took Leo to her sister's for two weeks, and I took some annual leave.

Bob and Will, the two workmen who came and rebuilt the ground floor of the house, were friends of a friend of

Tina's, and I felt duty bound to stay around and make sure they were doing the job properly. They were decent guys and I remember one day playing a Lou Rawls blues album and us all singing along to the songs for a whole afternoon. The house did look great after the work was done, and we had a new kitchen and completely redecorated ground floor. Needless to say, there was just one thing that was needed to set it all off, and that was yet another new sofa. However, I do remember some work colleagues popping round to the house one day just after it was all finished, and the looks on their faces told me that they were impressed with our house! I also had a happy wife, at least for a few weeks. I knew that I would have to find something else to cheer her up again before too long though. That was just the way things were.

Tina still loved shopping, and would often come home festooned with carrier bags after a day out in the town browsing the shops. There were three large wardrobes in the house, and they were all full. I had my clothes crammed into half of one of them, and Tina had her clothes packed into the rest of the space. She had clothes in several different sizes, as her size tended to fluctuate quite a lot. Every so often she would clear out her wardrobes and give her unwanted clothes to her daughter, Hannah, when they were speaking to each other. That was the way of their relationship. There would be weeks of not speaking, followed by a reconciliation, when they would often spend a whole day hugging each other on the sofa, then there would be an argument and we would go back to square one again. We were seeing more of Hannah as she was taking more of an interest in Leo again, something that I was determined to encourage.

Eventually, Hannah started having Leo with her on Saturdays, leaving Tina free to spend her day as she wished, as I usually worked Saturdays. There was work available most Saturdays on the charter trains, and then I would often work the Sunday as well. I stayed with a colleague in Hertfordshire to save me travelling backward and forward to Peterborough all weekend. Fred was also married to a difficult wife, and we would compare notes and sympathise with each other. Fred and I worked together during the week too, as he was my 'right-hand man' on the crew that I now had on the 08.00 King's Cross to Glasgow train. Fred and I had absolutely nothing in common apart from the fact that we were both in bad marriages. He had a daughter with his wife, and that was the reason why they were still together. He moved in and out of his wife's house often, as she used to give him a dog's life, as he put it, and he also had a flat in the village they lived in near Hatfield. I found myself seeking the company of other people who were in unhappy marriages so that we could share stories and find sympathy. I began to wonder if there were any people who were genuinely happily married. All the couples I ever saw seemed to be looking miserable, apart from the ones who had just met each other and hadn't had time to become disillusioned. I really was on a downer, but I thought that I had made my bed, so had I to lie in it.

One little incident seemed to sum up my life as the second year of my marriage to Tina wore on. One day, Tina came home with the customary collection of carrier bags hanging from her arms. She detached one bag and threw it over at me.

'There you are, don't say I never buy you anything!' she said, with her trademark cheeky smile.

I opened the bag, and inside was a striped shirt that I quite liked. I was just beginning to feel quite good about myself when I saw the receipt at the bottom of the bag. It was from the Oxfam shop. My loving wife had spent a small fortune on clothes for herself from the usual selection of High Street retailers, and had picked up a second hand shirt for me for £1.50.

I worked hard, long hours so that Tina could have more or less everything she wanted, and yet she could only manage to spend £1.50 on me. That really hurt, and was a nail in the coffin as far as our marriage was concerned. I remember telling my colleague Fred about it the next day, and having a hollow laugh with the rest of the team about it, but I was seriously unimpressed with my wife's idea of generosity.

Chapter 30

More Change at Work

I wasn't having a very successful time at home during the early 1990's, and to add to my miseries I was finding myself under more pressure at work too. We were constantly striving to improve customer service standards as the management felt we needed to compete with the airlines, and we were also being pressurised to take more money in catering revenue from our customers. I still had virtually no input into the team members that I had with me, and I was sick of members of staff being put on my team 'because I would be able to do something with them'. I remember one guy I had with me during this time, by the name of Paul. He would spend as much time as he possibly could sitting down. If I wanted him to do something, I had to ask him every time. He was incapable of thinking for himself; if I gave him more than one instruction at a time he would never remember the second task. He was with me for about three months. I later discovered that Paul had been put with me as a last resort. None of the other teams would tolerate him and they thought I could 'make something of him'.

The timetables changed in May, as they did every year, and I decided that I was going to go up and see my manager and ask what could be done about the quality of the staff I had on my team. The whole railway seemed to be populated with work-shy people at that time. I didn't seem to be able to find anyone who was capable of doing a decent day's work let alone looking after customers properly.

I made a special trip to London on my day off and went up to the office where the managers worked. They all knew me, and I was quite well-liked and respected by managers and staff alike after the years I had spent working on the railway.

'What can I do for you, Mr. Frost?' asked Andy, who was my direct boss. He was Scottish and usually called a spade a spade.

'It's like this, Andy,' I replied. 'I'm fed up with getting snotty letters from people at headquarters about the service on my train when you keep giving me idiots to work with!'

'What do you mean 'idiots'? asked Andy.

'Well, some of the staff I get aren't fit to clean the trains, let alone serve customers,' I replied.

The manager who was usually responsible for interviewing new staff discreetly left the office at this point. I think he was protecting himself from the firing line.

Andy finished what he was doing on the computer and turned to face me.

'OK,' he said. 'What do you want to do about it?'

I replied by giving him a list of the staff that I wanted on my team starting from the new May timetable. After I had read out my list, Andy totally surprised me by agreeing and saying that I could have every single one of the staff that I had asked for.

'They won't have a problem working with you and the hours should suit them all,' he said, 'so there's no problem with that.'

I was gobsmacked. It was the first time that I had ever gone into the office and asked for something. For fourteen years I had come to work, done my job, and gone home. I had never asked for any favours, never been in any trouble, never raised my head above the parapet before. I remember going over to the Great Northern Hotel and ordering a pint, even though it was only just after midday. I was over the moon. I was going to have the best team at King's Cross – now watch us go!

Fred, Keith the chef (I didn't like him, but he was a good chef), Joanna, Cathy, Christine, Danni and Sarah – they were all people that I had worked with before and I knew they would make a good team. They were responsible, took their jobs seriously, but also knew how to have a good time while working hard. I couldn't wait for the new regime to start. I went home and told Tina. She was pleased for me, but she did ask why I had requested so many attractive young women on the team!

'Why do you want all those pretty young girls on the crew'

'Because they're good workers, Tina. I hadn't even thought of what they look like'

I remember going into work the next day and telling the three lads that I had with me that they needed to look for other options for the new timetable. They were dumbfounded that I didn't want them, but I said that I was tired of having to tell them exactly what to do every day, and then following them around to see that it was done properly. I wanted people that I could rely on, and that was what I thought I had selected. I had taken a chance by telling the existing team that they were for the high jump, but they reacted quite well in the circumstances, and I did notice a slight improvement in their performance for the next week or two!

At around about the same time as this happened, I had a party of four railway staff reserved in my restaurant car for breakfast one day. They were joining the train at Peterborough and going to York, a journey of only just over an hour. The morning was extremely busy, and when we arrived at Peterborough, less than an hour from London, their table was not ready. They all went and sat at the dirty table, and I realised after a few minutes who they were and that they needed serving quickly. I went to the table and was surprised not to recognise any of them. They turned out to work for Human Resources, which was the new name for the Personnel Department. They were most unfriendly and were looking daggers at me for most of the time they were on the train, which was, fortunately, not very long. They had their breakfast and one of the party signed the bill. I thought that was the last I would ever see of them, but I was wrong. Two days later, I was called in to see my boss's boss, Ken Went. He was a very genuine and decent man, and it was usually a pleasure to see him.

This time was different, however. I walked into his office and he looked somewhat pained.

'Graham,' he said, 'I've had a bit of a complaint.'

'What's that about then?' I asked.

I had only ever had one written complaint from a customer in all my years on the railway. I was very proud of my record and concerned to hear about what had gone wrong.

'You remember you had a party of four from Human Resources on your train for breakfast from Peterborough to York the other day?' Ken continued.

'Yeah,' I replied. 'They were a right miserable lot, did nothing but sit there looking like they'd lost a pound and found a penny and then got off at York without even saying thank-you.'

'Well, they've complained,' said Ken. 'They say that the staff were most unwelcoming and that they had to sit at a dirty table when they got on the train at Peterborough.' Ken was looking even more pained now that he could see the expression on my face.

'I have to answer the complaint by the end of the week,' he went on.

I suggested, as calmly as possible, that perhaps he should tell them that as they were not paying for their breakfast, and as they were members of staff, they should have got up and helped out, or at least offered, instead of sitting there like royalty waiting to be served. Then to have the cheek to complain!

'I know,' replied Ken, sympathetically, 'but it doesn't work like that, unfortunately.'

I had to agree to let him say that I had been spoken to and that I had sent my apology. That wasn't what I wanted, and this little episode made me realise that if I was going to make a real difference to the way the railway was run I was going to have to come off the trains and go into management.

Three years later, three of the four people who had been in that party of four were made redundant when the new private railway company came in and realised that there were a lot of railway employees sitting in offices getting paid decent salaries for doing very little work. What goes around comes around!

It was very soon after the incident that I went for my first performance review with Ken. It was another sign that things were getting more business-like on the railway as I had never had a performance review before. In the railway industry people were promoted on seniority more often than not, and the only time you had to go and see a manager was if you had done something wrong. I really do wonder what some of the managers spent their time doing in those days, because they were rarely seen on trains and if you called them they always seemed to be in meetings. I remember my performance review well. I was scored from 1 to 6 on several areas of my performance. Ken had filled the form in before I got there, and it was my job to persuade him that he was wrong about me if I thought he had under-scored me on any of the points. Attendance was one point that I was scored on, and I remember that he had given me 5 out of 6.

'How can I only have five out of six?' I remonstrated. 'I haven't had a day off sick this year, in fact for two years. I have never been late, in fact I am always early for work and I have done loads of overtime.'

'Well, there is always room for improvement,' said Ken. 'That's what I believe. I am not scoring anyone six for anything.'

'That's ridiculous,' I replied. 'How can you improve on perfection?'

Well, that was his decision, and he stuck with it. I realised that there was no point in arguing any more. It was like talking to a brick wall, his mind was made up. He did say that he was very pleased with my performance and that he wished all his staff were like me, because then his job would be easier! I did feel rather let down by Ken after this exchange. Although he had said some really great things about me, he hadn't recognised me for what I thought was one of my greatest attributes, that I was always at work and always tried to give of my best. In those days, I used work as an escape from an increasingly unhappy home life, and I remember leaving that review meeting feeling that I wasn't really appreciated anywhere.

I realise now that he had probably been told by his own manager that he couldn't score anyone too highly as there was not sufficient money in the budget to pay too many top-rated bonuses.

I was to have cause to be thankful for my good relationship with Ken before too long.

Chapter 31

Marriage from Hell

By early 1994 I had accepted that I was trapped in a bad marriage. I looked at other people I knew who were in the same boat, like my sister-in-law Liz's husband Harry, and wondered if I could tolerate having a life like he had - forever. I didn't think I had much choice. Tina was a hypochondriac; I think she had a season ticket at the doctor's, and she was on endless pills for different ailments. She was a really unhappy person who always expected the worst and looked for the worst in people. I had tried to provide all the creature comforts that I thought she needed and still she was only happy for very brief periods. It got so bad that I would dread going home from work, because I always knew that she would be in a bad mood about something. I read in the newspaper one day about a new wonder-drug called Prozac, that was supposed to be the cure for depression. I went home and told Tina about it.

'Have you heard about this new anti-depression drug called Prozac, love? It's supposed to be the best thing since sliced bread'

'No, I haven't – the doctor hasn't mentioned it to me'

'Well, perhaps you might mention it the next time you are there, you never know, it might help you' s A few days later she had been to the doctor's and he had put her on Prozac. Her doctor had known her for years and I think he had got to the stage where he would give her what she wanted just to keep her quiet. I was getting near to that myself. After just over two years of marriage, I knew how he felt. If Tina didn't get her own way she could be very difficult, really unpleasantly difficult. And the Prozac didn't make any difference at all.

Several times I sat her down and tried to get to the bottom of what was making her so unhappy. I couldn't believe that it it was all because she was married to me, although I realised that I was not the man she needed in some areas of her life. Eventually she told me some very heavy stuff about having been seriously abused by one of her mother's partners when she was in her early teens. That had led her to have a number of violent and often very short-lived relationships during her life, and she had absolutely no self-esteem at all underneath all the bluster. She broke down and cried like a child; she told me that she had no idea how I put up with her, and that she didn't deserve someone like me, and that I deserved better. She couldn't understand how anyone could love her and she said the reason she treated me so badly was because she was trying to drive me to treat her badly, the way that most of the other men in her life had behaved. It was true that there had been times when I would walk out of the house because she made me so angry. I would sometimes jump in the car and go to a little pub on the road to Stamford, drink a couple of pints of bitter and drive back home. Despite the fact that I was totally against violence there were times when she would wind me up so much that I didn't trust myself not to react; I had to leave the house. Tina knew that, but she told me that there was something in her that just wanted all men to be evil.

All the mood swings, the hypochondria and the weight problems were related to that period of time in Tina's childhood. She told me that she had sought solace in drugs and alcohol over the years and had done many things that she was not proud of when she had been under the influence of different stimulants.

'I don't understand what possessed you to marry me, to be honest' she said. 'What would a nice bloke like you want with someone like me?'

I didn't know what to say. I just held her in my arms. There were a few times in our marriage when I thought there was a chance of moving things forward and creating a happy relationship, and this was one of them. I decided that I had to do everything that I could to make the marriage work. There was a tenderness between us immediately after that conversation that had been missing from our relationship for a very long time, and I really began to wonder if things were going to take a turn for the better.

By now I was working most Saturdays and as Hannah now had Leo on Saturdays, that left Tina with a free day, as she worked just on weekdays. She asked me if I minded her going to the pub for a few drinks with her cousin Andy on a Saturday afternoon. Again, I was flattered to be asked, as she normally just went ahead and did whatever she wanted to do, so I said that I didn't have a problem as long as she wasn't drunk when Hannah brought Leo back in the early evening. The last thing I wanted was for her to be looking after him whilst drunk, as I was often very late home on a Saturday night. Sometimes I didn't come home at all, and would stay nearer London with my colleague, Fred, if I was working an early train on the Sunday. I told her that I didn't have a problem with it as long as it was only for a couple of hours, she wasn't driving and it didn't affect Leo. I did have doubts, as a lot of the people who drank in our local pub, *The Horse and Groom,* had known Tina all her life, and I was sure that some of the men had been more than just friends with her in the past. You will have realised by now that Tina had a history of getting very drunk and not being responsible for her actions, and I didn't want her to slip back into that sort of behaviour again. Sometimes it was almost like being married to a child, although Tina was two-and-a-half years older than me. Her visits to *The Horse and Groom* became more frequent. If I had a Saturday off, I would go with her, although I had very little in common with the people who drank there. I felt a bit like a fish out of water there and wondered why some people found it necessary to spend so much time in the pub! I think Tina knew that I didn't really feel at home there. The only alternative activity that she would have been happy with on a Saturday would have been shopping, and I wasn't going to suggest that, as the whole idea of spending a day shopping with anyone is total anathema to me! Of course, it was only a few short years since most of my life had been spent in the pub, so it was an indication of how much I had already changed, and was still changing. I was quite happy to have a couple of cans of beer at home now.

Tina and I never went for a walk in the country the whole time we were together. I never suggested it because it never occurred to me that she would be interested. Our social life, such as it was, involved going to the pub, the very occasional meal out on one or other of our birthdays, and a rare party, either at our home or at the house of one of our friends.

Our home was a very pleasant place now. Although it was still a council house, we had transformed it from the, frankly, quite basic house that Tina had lived in when I first met her into a very comfortable home. We had satellite television and all the latest mod cons, and I was quite happy being the 'family man' and not going out very often. I loved spending time with Leo and I was always the one who got up in the night if he needed anything. I used to tell myself that at least I had him, and that I was thankful for the relationship we had. We didn't do anything special together, but I would play with him and his toys, and often took him out for walks on my day off during the week when Tina was at work.

Tina rarely worked a full week, even though she only worked three days a week. She often called in sick and, because I worked in the same place, it reflected on me. I was asked how she was all the time, by her managers and colleagues, and I felt embarrassed because I felt I had to lie.

People would stop me and say 'How's your Tina?'

I had to lie and say she wasn't very well at all, which on one level was true, but as far as her physical health was concerned she was perfectly well.

I couldn't bring myself to talk to Tina about it either, so it festered. The railway had recently introduced an absence policy, which meant that staff who were off sick had to have an interview with their manager when they returned. The railway was no longer prepared to pay people to sit at home and do nothing for months! It would prove to be the start of something that would completely transform our lives over the next year or so, but there was a lot more pain to go through first.

Chapter 32

Tenerife and a Big Birthday

Tina's cousin, Andy, and his wife, who also lived in Peterborough, had several weeks of timeshare apartments in Tenerife. I had been to Tenerife with my old friend, Jez, from work in 1986 and again in 1990, a few years later, not long before I met Tina. One day Tina said that Andy had invited us out to Tenerife for a week and all we would have to pay for was the flight and our spending money; the accommodation would be free. We just had to agree to look around a timeshare apartment and there would be no obligation to buy anything. Just a few weeks before that Tina had met someone who had told her that we could be millionaires in a few years if we got involved with an American network marketing business, and I had been very uncompromising in my refusal to get involved with that, so I thought I should give Tina the benefit of the doubt on the idea of the trip to Tenerife.

We flew out from Gatwick a few weeks later. Andy seemed to have brought half the *Horse and Groom* on this trip, and most of the men were drunk when we got on the plane. Some of them would stay that way for most of the week. Andy himself seemed to have an insatiable appetite for beer and made no secret of the fact that he spent between £100 and £200 in the pub every week. Andy and his wife had brought their two teenage children with them. The other two couples on the trip had come with just an appetite for a good time and plenty of alcohol. Even in my hard-drinking days, I had never really mastered the art of drinking in the daytime, apart from on Sundays. It appeared that I was going to have to be the responsible one on the trip as everyone else seemed to be headed for the bar as soon as possible after breakfast. Tina didn't need any encouraging in that area, and happily joined the rest of the group, leaving me with Leo.

I soon began to feel as if I was on the trip purely as a babysitter for Leo. We hardly went out of the timeshare complex in Los Cristianos for the entire week, apart from to visit a water park which, as a non-swimmer, was not really my idea of fun! It occurred to me that I had finally grown up and become responsible because I had a child to take care of, but that I was also being used in our relationship. The optimism I had felt surrounding me and Tina just a few short weeks earlier rapidly evaporated. Things became worse toward the end of the week when Tina did not even come back to our apartment for two consecutive nights. The excuse was that she was spending time with her family, but, as I pointed out, we lived less than a mile from them at home, but she had chosen not to have anything to do with them for years.

The day arrived when we were due to go and look around the timeshare apartment, as we had agreed before we set off on the trip. A perma-tanned salesman in white slacks with very white teeth took us around a number of apartments that had weeks available for sale. I was determined not to get sucked in to buying anything, but, as I might have expected, Tina had other ideas. A timeshare in Tenerife was just the sort of status symbol that would score points with Tina's sister, who, of course, had an apartment in Spain that she and her husband owned outright. Well, his family had been in the catering business in Bournemouth for three generations!

The next day was the penultimate day of our stay. I decided to go for one of my long walks, to decide whether or not I was going to succumb to this latest request from my wife. I walked from Los Cristianos to Playa de las Americas and back, a distance of some fifteen miles. I was deep in thought for most of the walk, stopping off for cups of coffee and to stare out to sea while I thought about the decision that I had to make. Time was, in my past, when I would have stopped off for a pint, but now it was coffee. A week in a timeshare cost over £3,000. I didn't have that much money in the bank so, if I agreed to Tina's request, I would have to borrow it. The only time in my life that I had ever borrowed money was to get the mortgage on my flat in London. I was in a quandary. I knew the bank would lend me the money, but I didn't want to borrow it. I didn't really want to be tied to coming to Tenerife for the same week every year, but Tina and Andy had told me that we could exchange our weeks and even go to other complexes all over the world if we wanted to. Above all, I didn't want to go home with an angry wife who would make my life a misery for the next few weeks and months if she didn't get her own way. So I caved in, and agreed to her request. I borrowed the money and bought the timeshare. It kept Tina happy for all of a week, as the little voice in my head had told me it would, and then she was off on another shopping spree to cheer herself up. I knew I couldn't keep this up forever, something had to change. Once we had the timeshare, Tina told all her friends about it and then realised that it would be almost a year before we could go out there and stay again.

When I went back to work after the Tenerife trip and spoke to some of my colleagues about my extravagant purchase they looked at me as if I was mad. I think, in a way, I was. I just did not seem to be able to return to the rational being I was before I got involved with Tina. Once again, I felt as if I was being dragged down a giant plughole, like a spider that has had the misfortune to find its way into a bath just as someone turns on the taps. There was one saving grace, however. Tina's cousin Andy had received a payment of £300 from the timeshare company as a reward for finding their new customer – me. He had the good grace to share that payment with me, which he didn't have to do, so that did soften the blow a little. I had arranged the bank loan with the minimum of fuss, now I just had to organise the household budget to cover the repayments on the loan. Tina had also got herself a credit card around this time without telling me, and had run up several hundred pounds worth of debt, which she expected me to help her to pay off. I refused, however, saying that she could either have the timeshare or the debt paid off, but not both.

I was feeling a little guilty for having refused to help her with her debt a few days later, as I walked down the road near our house and I saw a shiny red Ford Escort for sale. Tina's fortieth birthday was fast approaching and I had been thinking of buying her a car as a present. I hardly ever got to use 'our' car and was still taking taxis to and from the station to get me to work and back. I worked out that it would be as cheap for me to buy Tina her own car, over a period of two years, so I went home and suggested that she might like to come and take a look at the shiny red Ford Escort. It was quite old, but in excellent condition, and she was quite overwhelmed that I was thinking of buying it for her. She told me that she didn't deserve me, for probably the hundredth time, and I melted yet again and realised why I still loved her, despite all our difficulties. I explained to her that I would pay for the car but that the running costs would be her responsibility and that she was not to come to me for the money for insurance, tax and fuel. She agreed quite willingly and we went and saw the person selling the car and made the purchase. It was competitively priced and did not break the bank! I also meant that I was able to drive myself to the station every day and I had a car to use on my rare days off without having to share with Tina.

I bought the car for Tina several weeks before her fortieth birthday, so that when the actual day of her birthday came around I bought her a new camera, just to surprise her. She was totally surprised as she had not been expecting a second present. Major brownie points for me! Tina's sister and niece had come down for a few days to help her celebrate but I made myself scarce at work for most of the time as I still didn't get on very well with Liz, my sister-in-law.

We had a small party in a local pub for Tina's 40th and a lot of the old friends showed up. Not surprisingly, we had not seen most of them since the last time we had been providing the booze and food for free. I had an enjoyable evening, Tina was happy being the centre of attention and the party passed off without any major incident. I enjoyed seeing my wife happy and managed to have a few drinks and enjoy myself too. I was once again flavour of the month with my wife, at least for a week!

Chapter 33

Light at the end of the Tunnel?

Soon after Tina's fortieth birthday her boss started expressing concern about the amount of time she took off work sick. We worked for different departments by this time as Tina had taken a job on King's Cross station and was, supposedly, working full time. However, she rarely completed a full week and the trips to the doctor had become even more frequent. Eventually, her boss wrote to her and asked if he could come and see her on a 'home visit'. I advised her to accept, and an appointment was made for a day when I would be there to support her. The day arrived and I drove to Peterborough station to meet her boss off the train. John was a decent sort of fellow who had worked on the railway for many years. I knew him reasonably well and we chatted amicably on the two-mile drive from Peterborough station to our house. When we arrived I could immediately see that Tina was going to put on some sort of dying swan act. I had left her looking perfectly all right, now here she was sitting on the sofa looking as if she had the weight of the world on her shoulders. As soon as John sat down and asked her how she was feeling, she burst into floods of uncontrollable tears.

She managed to convey to John that the reason she was in such a state was because 'her marriage was breaking down and there was nothing that she could do about it.' John and I looked at each other dumbfounded, and after a few moments he asked me if I would mind taking him back to the station. I was only too happy to oblige, and we consoled each other on the drive back to the station about how we would never understand women if we lived to be a hundred years old! I was aware that John had a partner who he found challenging, so was pretty sure that the events of the last half-an-hour would not be broadcast around the railway family too much, as people who live in glass houses rarely throw stones, if they have their wits about them!

It was just one of the occasions during my time with Tina that I was completely dumbfounded. I drove back to the house and asked her why she had decided to tell her boss what she hadn't even told me, in other words that she was worried that our marriage was breaking down.

'Whatever possessed you to come out with all that?' I asked.

'Well, you're never here, and when you are, you aren't interested in me. Not really. You never have been. I don't know why you married me because you don't want to be with me. I can't remember the last time you told me that you loved me.'

And so it went on. Fortunately, Tina's manager John went back to London and walked straight into the Human Resources manager's office. Ron, the HR Manager, was a decent sort, and arranged for Tina to have some counselling at the company's expense in the hope that this would encourage her to return to work. After her next day at work she came home and informed me that her manager had arranged for her to go to see a counsellor in London once a week. I was very pleased and thought that this could be the start of some real progress for us as a couple. Tina suggested that I might talk to someone about my past and the effect it was having on my present, as it were, so I readily agreed to seek some help, in the hope that it would move our relationship forward.

I made an appointment at the doctor's, for the first time since I had been cured of cancer in 1980. I explained a little about my upbringing to the doctor and that I believed it was affecting my relationship with Tina. After a few moments of thought he agreed to refer me to a therapist in one of the Peterborough hospitals. A couple of weeks later I went along to meet this therapist, whose name was Derek. He was rather a severe-looking man in his mid-forties, with a trimmed beard, dressed in a sports jacket and trousers. I was to be part of a therapy group that would meet every Tuesday morning from 10 until 11 am. We were not to have anything to do with each other outside of the room we met in, were not allowed to give each other lifts to the hospital or have any contact outside of the actual group. I was willing to try anything to make my relationship with Tina work, so agreed to all the conditions of membership of this therapy group. It caused huge problems at work because all my Tuesday shifts had to be covered and the young lady who administered all the rosters was far from happy, especially when she was told that the reason for my need to have every Tuesday off was confidential and she wasn't allowed to know!

I went to my first group therapy session. There were eight of us, four women and four men. We sat in a circle on what I call 'chapel chairs' – those hard wooden chairs with pockets in the back for religious materials. It was very much like being back in the religious meetings of my youth and I found it very disconcerting. I remember there was one man there who constantly went on about how life was really only about sex and money. He was there because his wife was having an affair, although he did eventually admit that he was as well. I said that I was there because my marriage was not working and I would do almost anything to make it work. After the first meeting I was rather underwhelmed but thought I had better give it three or four attempts before I made any judgements. I really wanted some magic formula that was going to give me a happy marriage, as I knew that things couldn't continue as they were for much longer.

Approaching the hospital for the second group therapy meeting I saw one of the girls from the group and greeted her with a 'Good morning.'

'You're not supposed to talk to me outside the group' she said, with a strange light in her eyes. I found this rather worrying, as she then went straight into the group and told Derek, the facilitator, that I had approached her in the street and said 'Good morning'! I felt like a naughty schoolboy and started mentally questioning the authenticity of this system of therapy. I did go back for the third session, but my mind was made up after the second session. Half the group members didn't say anything because they 'weren't ready'. I am one of those people who jumps in with both feet when I have an opportunity like that, so I didn't have much patience with people who appeared to have been attending the group for months but had not taken any benefit from it.

Nadine, the roster clerk at work, was delighted when I went back to her and said that I was now available on Tuesdays again.

Chapter 34

Eureka!

Tina came home from one of her counselling sessions with Sarah, her counsellor in London, and said that she thought I should go and see her as well. Sarah was a private counsellor and I had no idea of how much it would cost to see her, but Tina persuaded me to go and see Ken, my boss, to ask him if he would fund some counselling for me.

'But, Graham,' he said, when I went to see him a couple of days later, 'you're a model employee! You never take any time off work, you're always here, why would you need counselling?'

I explained to him that I was having some pretty severe problems with my marriage and that my wife felt it would be beneficial to me if I went and saw the same counsellor as she was seeing. I asked Ken if he could fund a few sessions for me and I would report back to see if I had found it helpful. He agreed, with some reluctance, and I left him to make the necessary arrangements with Human Resources.

My first appointment with Sarah was a fortnight later. I had gone along with Tina. The idea was that we would spend some time with Sarah together and then we would have half-an-hour each on our own. Sarah lived in a large house in North London, where she had a consulting room on the first floor. My first impression of Sarah was that she was kind, friendly and genuine. When I had my half-hour alone with her, I just poured out my heart to her. The half-hour seemed like five minutes. She just listened, and gently drew me to a close just before the half-hour was completed. Sarah asked me to write her a brief précis of my early life before attending the next session, which was booked in for a week later, and on a different day to Tina's appointment. Sarah was also keen to ensure that I wouldn't have to take time off work to attend the appointments with her. She told me that these times were to be 'my time', and that I should try to spend the journey to North London to see her on my own thoughts and dreams. I left that first appointment feeling as if a huge weight had been lifted from my shoulders. I hadn't even started to tell Sarah the story of how I had arrived where I was in life, but I had an overwhelming feeling that I had found the place where I was going to find the solution to my problems. It was as if I had started building a new house and had just laid the first brick.

Over the next few weeks, Sarah heard my whole life story, including all the personal bits that I had always shied away from telling anyone. I felt that I had an opportunity for a fresh start here, and I wasn't going to waste it. For the first two one-hour appointments, Sarah just sat and listened, and nodded, and occasionally asked me how I had felt about something or how I was feeling about it now. Every time I left her house, I felt a little better about myself. I began to remember who I had been before I met Tina, and to realise that there hadn't been much wrong with that person after all. Sarah encouraged me to use the time that I spent travelling from Peterborough to north London and back as 'me time', to think about the things that I wanted to do with my life in the future. I still had just about enough hair to warrant a visit to the barber's in those days, and there was an old-fashioned Greek barber's shop on the corner of the road where Sarah lived. I would go in there once a month for a 'number 2' hair cut and a scalp massage. The shop was tiny and run by two very elderly Greek brothers. The décor was very primitive – I suspect that nothing had changed about that shop in twenty or thirty years. There was an orange box to put my feet on when I was sitting on the barber's chair, and the Greek brothers would always ask their customers if they wanted 'something for the weekend' with a twinkle in their eye. I used to sit there and ruefully wish that I had a need for 'something for the weekend' as the physical side of my relationship with Tina had never really got going, and was certainly completely non-existent by the time I started going to see Sarah.

I came to look forward to my weekly appointments with Sarah enormously. I hoped that Tina would be able to find some way of moving forward through her conversations with Sarah too, and there was a slight change to begin with, but it soon became apparent that I was the one moving forward without her. I still loved her, but it was beginning to dawn on me that the reality is there is no point in loving someone who doesn't love you back. Actually, the truth was even more painful than that. I loved someone who didn't know how to love, at least, not in the way that I needed loving. I realised over a period of a few months that I was staying in the relationship with Tina for Leo's benefit, effectively using him as an excuse for staying put. It took a long time for Sarah to help me to realise that he was not, in fact, my responsibility, as he was not my child. I was slowly destroying myself and using Leo as an excuse. In the long term, that would be extremely damaging for both of us. I couldn't have loved that little boy more if he had been my own flesh and blood, but I knew in my heart of hearts that I wasn't helping him in the long term by bringing him up in an unhappy home.

Sarah was an excellent counsellor, and rarely slipped out of the 'questioning' mode, but one day, after several months of my weekly sessions, she said, 'Graham, you really are going to have to find a way of making yourself accept that your relationship with Tina is going nowhere and you have to start looking for a way of escaping and getting your life back.'

Sarah was a very experienced and practised counsellor who had spent a lot of time counselling Second World War veterans who were suffering from Post Traumatic Stress Disorder. She had an uncanny knack of making me believe that everything was going to be all right again. She was her husband's second wife and they had a ten-year old son. I trusted her implicitly and told her everything.

A few months after I started my counselling sessions with Sarah, Tina stopped going to see her altogether and had slipped back to many of her old ways, including taking a lot of time off work and going out with her friends on a Saturday night without telling me where she was going, or indeed, that she was going out at all. I got home from work on a Saturday night to find Leo with a babysitter at least twice a month. Tina would be out nightclubbing with her friends, and would come in during the early hours of the morning, reeking of alcohol. One day she sat me down and asked if we could stay together but live separate lives.

'I just think it would be better if we carry on living together but do our own thing most of the time' she said.

'What do you mean? I asked

'Well, you never come near me any more. You obviously don't want to be with me really, so why don't we just live separate lives?

'Well' I said, 'I'm not prepared to do that. As far as I'm concerned we are either together as husband and wife or we are not together at all. You want the security of having me here but the freedom to do whatever you want. It doesn't work like that, Tina, not for me'. As happened so often in our relationship, we finished a conversation because neither of us liked the idea of where the conversation was going. Going to see Sarah had made me see what was obvious to many other people, that our relationship was doomed.

A couple of weeks before Christmas 1994, Tina announced that she was going out with her friends for a pre-Christmas girls' night out on a Friday evening. I was working, as usual, and she had arranged for Laura, our usual babysitter, to look after Leo for the evening. I advised her to get a taxi into town, rather than taking her car, and resigned myself to her coming in at 3am reeking of alcohol again. Perhaps I was turning into a boring husband, but I considered that as I had completely changed my social habits since I had married Tina, I could reasonably expect her to tone it down a bit too! Of course, while she was out partying with her friends, she could forget her responsibilities and the fact that she was in an unsatisfactory marriage. Work was my escape, and I often deceived myself with the story that I worked so many hours because we needed the money.

I arrived home from work that Friday evening at about 9.30pm, and noticed that Tina's car was missing from outside the house. I thought exasperatedly to myself that she had ignored my advice and gone out in the car after all. Well, I hoped she would have the sense to leave the car in town and get a taxi home. I paid Laura and thanked her, making sure that she got home safely before I went up to check on Leo. He was sleeping peacefully so I went downstairs, opened a can of beer, made myself a sandwich and sat down to watch television. By 11.30 I was dropping off to sleep in the chair, having been up since 4 am, so I decided to head off to bed. I checked on Leo again; he was still fast asleep. I went to bed and was asleep within minutes. At 2.30am the bedside phone rang. It was one of Tina's friends, Jackie.

'Graham, it's Jackie. So sorry to ring you at this time of night but it's Tina. She's been arrested. We're at the police station. She's been picked up for drinking and driving. Can you come and get her?'

'OK, Jackie,' I replied, 'tell her that I said she has got herself into the police station, so she can damn well get a taxi home. There is no way that I am going to get out of bed, wake Leo up and get him in the car to come down there at this time of night.'

Jackie went very quiet at the other end of the line. Tina's friends were used to me doing whatever she wanted.

'OK, I'll tell her,' she said.

I didn't envy Jackie that task. Tina was inclined to get a bit stroppy when she had a few drinks in her and I knew some of her friends were a little wary of her.

I stayed in bed, but inside I was boiling. How could she be so irresponsible? It wasn't as if she couldn't afford a taxi in to town. It would have cost Tina and her friends a pound each from our house into town, and the same to come back. I was angrier than I had been for a long time. I went downstairs for a cigarette, trying to think of what I was going to say to her when she got home. If it wasn't for Leo there was no question but that this would have been the final nail in the coffin where our relationship was concerned. I couldn't bring myself to leave him with her, because she was so obviously not fit to bring up a child. What a mess I had got myself into, and how was I ever going to extricate myself from it without hurting anyone? I went back to bed, and Tina arrived home soon after. She came up to bed after a while and crept around the bedroom, trying not to wake me, I guessed. After a few moments she got into bed beside me.

'Are you awake?' she whispered.

'Yes, I'm awake. How could I possibly sleep when my wife has been arrested for drunken driving?'

'I'm really, really sorry. I know you must be really angry with me.'

'Angry? I'm furious, Tina. How could you be so irresponsible? You have a child in the next room that you are responsible for, never mind me! What would happen to him if you had had an accident and been killed? You never think of the consequences of your actions on others.'

It struck me, yet again, that I was speaking as if I had been scolding a child. She had no sense of responsibility for herself, let alone anyone else. Part of me still wanted to take care of her, but I was increasingly understood that taking care of her was taking too big a toll on who I was, and that I was neglecting myself terribly while concentrating on her. It turned out that she had been driving along one of the main streets in Peterborough with the sunroof on the car open, in December, stereo blaring and singing at the top of her voice. She was two-and-a half times over the legal alcohol limit for driving. She tried to hug me and was very apologetic that night, but I didn't want any of it. There is nothing less attractive than a drunk partner, unless you are drunk yourself, and I was in no mood for physical contact with Tina that night. A few weeks later she went to court – I resolutely refused to go with her, and was fined and banned from driving for three years. Another nail in the coffin of our relationship.

Chapter 35

The End Approaches

At about the same time as Tina's drink driving charge, the
HR Manager, Richard, called me in to his office one day.

'Graham,' he said, 'we are having to review the funding of
counselling services, and I'm afraid we won't be able to
fund your sessions with Sarah any more after next month.'

I was horrified, and wondered what the solution to this
problem might be. I rang Sarah, and she told me not to
worry, we could talk about it at our next session. She
kindly offered to continue with the sessions, and I could
pay her 'what I could afford'. I continued with the sessions
and left a financial contribution for Sarah each time.

Christmas came closer. I had put my foot down and said
that I was not going to fund the usual Boxing Day
gathering of all Tina's friends, that one of her friends could
host something on Boxing Day for a change.

Unsurprisingly, nothing came of that idea! On Christmas morning, I prepared our usual breakfast of smoked salmon and scrambled egg with Buck's Fizz, and took it up to the bedroom. I then went downstairs leaving Tina, Hannah and Leo to open their presents and spend some rare time together as a family. I busied myself preparing lunch, a task I enjoyed very much. I had some music on and was in my own little world. After a while, Tina and Hannah brought Leo downstairs to play with his new toys.

Tina came into the kitchen to chat. 'Graham, do you mind if Hannah and I meet up with some friends at the pub?'

'Do you have to, Tina? Can't we spend Christmas morning together? Why don't you play with Leo?'

'But I told Jackie and the girls that we'd meet them before lunch. Just for an hour or so. Please?'

'Well, I can't leave the lunch now. Go on, then,' I said, not very graciously, 'but make sure you're home by 1pm.'

'Thank you,' Tina said, twirling out of the kitchen in yet another new outfit bought on one of her recent shopping expeditions.

I carried on with the cooking, and kept an eye on Leo. By 3 pm I was getting concerned that the lunch was going to be ruined, and Leo was asking where his mum and nanny were. I rang Tina's mobile phone and got no reply. Eventually they turned up at 4pm, both as drunk as lords. Leo and I had eaten our Christmas lunch together by then. Once again I was furious, but this time there was no apology from Tina.

'Well, I don't get much chance to spend time with my daughter, do I? You don't begrudge me a few drinks with my daughter, do you?'

I thought it imprudent to start an argument with Hannah and Leo there. I was angrier than I had ever been in my life, something that was becoming a regular occurrence. However, I was determined not to let her get to me. Tina had once admitted that she thought all men were 'bastards', and that she goaded them to prove that. There was no way that I was going to give her the satisfaction of being able to say that I was just the same as some of the violent men she had been with before she met me. I knew I was better than that. I also knew that I was reaching the end of my tether in the whole situation. I had poured so much of myself into caring for Tina and Leo that I had completely lost sight of my own life.

Early in 1995, I had a Saturday off work, and agreed with Tina that I would go to the pub with her in the afternoon. I had got out of the habit of regular heavy drinking, and after an hour or two in the pub, I wondered what I had seen in that sort of lifestyle for so many years. I remembered the days when I had thought there was something wrong with people who never went to the pub. Now there I was asking myself what was so great about people who spent most of their leisure time drinking in their local! That particular pub was frequented by the locals from the 'village' just down the road from where we lived. It wasn't really a village any more, as it had become part of the greater city of Peterborough, but it was easy to see how it had once been a small village on the outskirts of Peterborough. Most of the men who drank in there had lived around the area all their lives, several of them had gone to school with Tina and I'm sure more than one of them had had a relationship with her over the years. They weren't really my sort of people, probably because I felt a little threatened by them. Tina was in her element, knocking back the pints twice as quickly as I was, and acting like one of the boys.

One of the regulars came up to me and asked me how I had got mixed up with Tina. I told him that I had met her at work, and explained our relationship in as few words as I could.

'Well, you must be a good feller,' he said 'taking on the young lad and all. She's a bit of a girl, you know, your Tina!'

I asked him what he meant.

'Well, she's down here every Saturday afternoon, drinking like a fish' he said, 'and when she runs out of money, she's on the scrounge for drinks. She even nicks other people's drinks when they're not looking. You need to watch her, mate.'

I was furious, a feeling that was more and more familiar. When we finally got home late that afternoon, Leo was out with Hannah and I was hungry. We decided to order a Chinese takeaway, and we sat eating it in the lounge, watching television. I had to tell Tina what I was feeling.

'You're an absolute disgrace, Tina! I shouted. 'How can you carry on like that down at the pub when I'm not around? You should be thoroughly ashamed of yourself. What sort of an example are you setting your daughter – it's no wonder she's such a mess when she has you for a mother! - I'm ashamed of you – whatever possessed me to marry someone like you..?' She had never seen me that angry, because I had always controlled myself before and internalised the anger. Sarah, my counsellor, had taught me that to internalise anger in that way was very bad for me and would be very likely to lead to stress-related illness. In the end, Tina left her Chinese food and disappeared upstairs to bed. I heard her crying, but resisted the temptation to go and comfort her. Enough was enough, I told myself, justifying my outburst to myself. I had never been so verbally vicious to anyone in my entire life. All my pent-up anger and resentment had come out in a few sentences of absolute vitriol. I knew things were coming to a head.

The next week, on the early morning train to London for work, I talked to one of the girls on my team who travelled in to work with me every day. Christine knew me quite well, and she was aware that all was not well between Tina and I. All my workmates knew that my marriage was unhappy, but they diplomatically kept quiet about it, apart from when my back was turned, I'm sure. This particular morning Christine said something that unknowingly provided me with a lifeline.

'You know I've got a house in Peterborough that's rented out, don't you?' she asked.

'Yes,' I replied.

'Well, if you wanted to rent it, the tenants I have in there at the minute, their contract is up in a couple of months.'

I thanked her, and went very quiet. We used to try and catch some sleep on the train to work in the morning, as we had to get up at 3.30am to catch that train, and we wouldn't be home until 9pm. I'm sure I closed my eyes that morning, but I wouldn't have slept, because the idea of a life free from Tina began to look like more of a reality. What would I do? I had no idea, but just the opportunity to have my own life again was worth dreaming about. Of course, I still had my flat in Brixton Hill, but moving back there after nearly four years in the comparative calm of Peterborough wasn't an attractive prospect. I had lost touch with all my London friends and had no wish to be alone in London again. In Peterborough, I felt, I could re-build my life. I had started on the path back to having my own life again.

Chapter 36

Leo and Hannah

I had made my mind up that I was going to leave Tina, but it was going to be an enormous wrench for me to leave Leo. I often used to say that I couldn't have loved Leo more if he had been my own child. No matter how busy I was with work, I would always make time to spend one day a week with him. When he was really small, perhaps just over a year old, I had fallen asleep on the sofa momentarily when I was supposed to be looking after him one afternoon. He had toddled out into the kitchen and opened a cupboard door. Tina used to keep all her make-up in a box in the cupboard under the sink, and he found the box and plastered himself in make-up. I woke up and wandered out into the kitchen to see where he was. I'm ashamed to say that I picked him up and smacked him. It was just a reaction and I am unsure where it came from. A few hours later, when I was ruminating on my actions, I realised that this had come from my father and the one and only time he had ever hit me. I felt so bad about the incident that I continued to apologise to Leo about it until he was 12 or 13. It took me an hour, and a lot of struggling and swearing in my head, to get the make-up off his face, and the clothes he was wearing were ruined.

Leo had started at nursery school when he was four years old, and it had often fallen to me to take him to the nearby nursery. I tried to persuade him to walk, but as often as not he would end up riding on my shoulders. When I went to collect him he would run out of the school like a bullet out of a gun and come to me for a hug.

One day when someone asked him what he wanted to when he grew up, he said, 'I want to wear funny clothes and work on a train, like Papa.'

The funny clothes were a reference to the uniform I wore. When I heard him say that I was so proud I nearly burst into tears. Someone wanted to be like me!

I had taken my substitute father role very seriously over the past four years but realised that I could still be a part of his life, even if I wasn't living under the same roof. However, in order to achieve that, I knew that I had to start trying to build a relationship with Hannah. By that time, Hannah had a small flat in another part of Peterborough. She had cleaned up her life and was ready to try and have Leo back in her life. I needed to know if I was going to support that process, or recommend that Leo stay with Tina. I wasn't sure if Tina would be able to cope with a small, demanding child without me around to take off some of the pressure, and I felt that I owed it to Leo to make sure that he was cared for as well as possible if I wasn't going to be around so much. I started going round to see Hannah once or twice a week, and I didn't tell Tina where I was going. After a couple of visits Hannah really opened up to me and told me some stories about her childhood that made me very thankful for the fact that I had been brought up in a loving and secure home, albeit a very restrictive one. I knew Tina had a chequered past, but the stories Hannah recounted to me were disturbing. Her mother had had one violent relationship after another and Hannah had witnessed her mother being beaten on more than one occasion. She also revealed to me that her mother had regularly left her alone from Thursday evening until Sunday when she had been out on one of her benders. I had been trying not to think about Tina's past and all these revelations made me realise just exactly who I had married. All in all, it was no wonder that Hannah had left home and put herself into care at the age of 14. That was the story she gave me; to this day I have no idea whose version of events was closest to the truth.

One evening I arrived home from work at about 10 pm, after having been to visit Hannah on my way home from work. I felt that I really wanted to help her, that she had been treated most unjustly by her mother, and that I was the right person to start making some sort of amends for all her problems. Unusually for Tina, she wasn't in front of the television, and then I heard her on the phone upstairs. She was talking to her sister, Liz.

'I think he's seeing someone else. He never gets home from work until 10 at the earliest, and he just ignores me most of the time.' There was a gap while Liz said something. I resisted the temptation to pick up the downstairs phone so that I could hear what was being said.

'I have let myself go a bit, to be honest Liz, I'm bigger than I have ever been and it's no wonder he doesn't fancy me any more.'

I was shocked that Tina even cared what I thought of her. The conversation with Liz went on for quite a few minutes longer and then I could hear Tina crying. I had seen crocodile tears from her before, and I was determined that I was not going to give in again. I had realised that I was trapped in a marriage that was never going to work, and I now had an opportunity to get out. Nothing Tina could say or do now was going to change my resolve that 'out' was the only place to be. The very idea that she thought I was having an affair with someone else!

After a few minutes Tina came downstairs.

'How long have you been in?' she asked.

'Not very long,' I replied evasively. 'Are you OK?'

'Yeah, I'm OK,' she replied, not very convincingly, and went out to the kitchen to get herself a drink. I will never know if she had heard me come in to the house during that conversation with her sister or not.

Chapter 37

The End is Nigh

The next day I as I travelled in to King's Cross for work again Christine, my colleague, asked if I was still interested in renting her house.

'My tenants are moving out in three weeks,' she said. 'It's yours if you want it!'

I didn't even stop to draw breath.

'Yes, please, I'll take it,' I replied, then swallowed nervously, realising what a huge decision I had just made. I had just decided to leave my wife, something I had thought I would never do, something I had criticised others for doing. However, I immediately felt much better just for having made the decision, and that day's trip to Glasgow and back passed very quickly. I already felt as if I was walking on air!

When I arrived home that evening, I bounced into the house and couldn't wait to give Tina my news. She was sitting disconsolately in front of the television when I arrived . As usual, she paid scant attention to me when I walked through the door.

'Tina, I have something to tell you,' I said, before I had even taken off my coat. 'I am leaving you. I have found somewhere else to live and I'm moving out in three weeks' time.'

A look of pure anger and vengefulness came over her face.

'Well, you'll be sleeping on the sofa for three weeks then,' she said. 'I'm not having you in my bed.'

What followed was the worst three weeks of the time we had been together. I tried to make it as normal as possible for Leo's benefit. I had to find a way of explaining to him that I was leaving, but life was far from easy for those weeks. Tina didn't speak to me at all, and carried on as if I was already gone. I realised that I should have kept my news until the day before I was going, but I am too honest in these situations and I really felt it best that she knew as soon as I had made the decision.

I decided that I was not going to give Tina the opportunity to bad mouth me after I had gone – I made sure all the household maintenance tasks were done and the garden tidy before I left. I even hired a chainsaw and trimmed back the trees in the garden! I ensured that all the bills were paid up to date and that there was food in the freezer. No-one was going to accuse me of deserting my wife with nothing.

The previous tenants of the small house that I was moving into ended up moving out a few days early, and that gave me the opportunity to take Leo round and show him the house before I moved in. It was a tiny, one-bedroomed house on the other side of Peterborough from where I was living with Tina. Leo was not quite five years old, and the only father figure he had known was leaving him. I wasn't at all comfortable with that, but I had, through my sessions with Sarah, and my own knowledge of myself, come to the conclusion that leaving Tina and Leo was the only course of action open to me, if I was to retain my sanity.

Three days before my moving date, I put Leo in the car and drove him over to my new home. I opened the door and we went in to a completely unfurnished house.

'Papa is moving into this house soon' I said. Nan and Papa haven't been getting on very well and we have decided that we can't live together any more. I will still see you all the time and you can come and stay over here sometimes, but I will be living here all the time. I still love you very much and I always will'.

As I was saying those words I was wondering how many other people were saying similar things to children they loved that day, and how many of them would keep their word. I knew I would always be there for Leo.

I was close to tears myself, and Leo looked at me very solemnly, as he looked around the empty house.

'What are you going to sit on, Papa?' he asked.

Well, I will have to buy some furniture and some of my friends are going to lend me an old sofa to sit on so I will be ok', I said, touched beyond measure that he was more concerned about me than he was about himself.

Over the next few days I kept as low a profile at home as I could. Tina was not at all happy about my imminent departure, despite the fact that she had so obviously been unhappy for most of the time we had lived together. My one act of defiance was to take her car with me. As I saw it, she still had two years before she would be allowed to drive again, so I might as well get some use from the car.

'By the way, I'm taking your car when I go. There's no point in leaving it here, you can't drive it for another two years'

'You can't do that, it's my car, you bastard, you're not taking my car!'

'You have no say in the matter, Tina' I replied, calmly, although I wasn't feeling calm. I was feeling a mixture of anger and exhilaration.

'I'm taking the car and that's the end of it. I am leaving you better off than when I met you. You have a lovely home, no debts and you're banned from driving so there's no point in you having a car'.

After that exchange of words, I was surprised that Tina instigated a few moments of tenderness between us the evening before I left, then she announced that she was taking Leo down to stay with her sister for a few days while I moved out. I was left to move out on my own, which I preferred. I had very little in the way of possessions to show for my three years with Tina. I had decided to take none of the furniture or domestic appliances with me, as the house I was moving into was tiny, and of course I still had my London flat, which was rented out fully furnished. Two car loads of records, books, clothes and other possessions and it was done. My first priority was to get a television and hi-fi, as Tina and I had combined our stereo systems and I had decided to leave the resulting stereo system with her. I bought a cheap second-hand portable television and a not-so-cheap second-hand stereo system the same day I moved. I find it impossible to live without music and I thought I would need the television for company as I was not used to living alone now!

I had borrowed an old sofa from Richard and Sophie, friends from work, and after I had unpacked everything and set up the television and stereo I sat down and relaxed. It was early on a Saturday evening, and I was free again. I could go back to having my own life, without having to worry about what mood the person I was living with was in when I woke up every morning. It was a tremendous relief to have control over my own life again and I enjoyed the peace.

Soon, I would start to plan the rest of my life, but for a while, it was time to relax a little and remember who I had been five years earlier. Perhaps he hadn't been such a bad person after all. Now what was I going to do with the rest of my life?

Graham Frost now runs Heart-Shaped Decisions CIC with his colleagues David Hyner and Mark Wingfield.

They specialise in helping people between the ages of 15 and 25 improve their confidence and self-esteem in order to build fulfilled and productive lives.

Heart-Shaped Decisions CIC works in schools, colleges, universities and prisons, and seeks donations, sponsorships and partnerships to support our work. The profit from sales of this book, and Graham's other books, goes to support the work of Heart-Shaped Decisions CIC. Please contact Graham graham@grahamfrost.com or on 07766 916317 if you would like to know more about how you can support us.

https://www.heartshapeddecisions.com

There will be a third book in 2025..

Here is a taste of the first chapter of 'Further Forward'..

My first few days in the tiny rented house I had moved into after leaving Tina were a blessed relief. I had decided not to drink any alcohol for the first month in my new home, as I was conscious that I might fall into the trap of drowning my sorrows. I was still driving to the station to get the train to work, so that put paid to drinking after work. I had also resolved that I was not going to look for another relationship for at least a year. There were going to be some differences in the life of the post-Tina me!

I had bought a second hand hi-fi system and an old Grundig 14" portable television, so had all the home entertainment that I needed. I listened to Bonnie Raitt's 'Road Tested' live CD a lot those first few days and weeks, and had difficulty controlling the tears when I heard the ballad 'Matters of the Heart'

Broken heart, bloodshot stare
Signs of a fool who cared too much
Now she's gone and he can't remember how
To live without her touch
Hopin' to die but surely livin' to tell

When it comes to matters of the heart

There is nothing a fool won't get used to

So he found someone afraid his heart would follow the heat
He could hardly do more than pretend
Though she knew in her heart that his love was alive

When it comes to matters of the heart
There is nothing a fool won't get used to

Now of all the things love teaches
All the ways that it opens our eyes
None more profound than the lesson he learned
The day she walked out of his life
Well when the road gets too narrow
It's then he remembers her smile
And he sees these words forming on her lips
Across a river of tears he once cried

When it comes to matters of the heart
There is nothing a fool won't get used to

(Michael McDonald)

The song was written by Michael McDonald, formerly of
the great 1970's band 'The Doobie Brothers' but Bonnie
Raitt has the best version of it, in my opinion. Part of me
knew that I had done everything in my power to make my
marriage to Tina work, but I still felt, for some unknown
reason,that I had failed.

I went to see Sarah, my counsellor in London, during that first week alone, and told her that I had been listening to the Bonnie Raitt song. She told me that I wasn't a fool, and that I hadn't got used to anything, because I was free to do whatever I wanted to now. It was still a long time before I could listen to Van Morrison's 'Have I Told You Lately' without a tear or two. That had been 'our song' when Tina and I had first been together.

At the end of my first week in my new home, I developed a terrible stomach pain. I always think these things are going to go away on their own, but it persisted, so I spoke to Hannah, my stepdaughter. We had become quite close and she was fully supportive of my decision to leave her mother. After a day or two of pain, I decided that I needed to go to the hospital. I have never enjoyed dealing with medical professionals, despite the fact that they saved my life when I was 24, but I knew the pain wasn't going away so decided to seek help. Hannah came with me to the hospital.

I was admitted with suspected appendicitis. Within an hour or two I was hooked up to a drip and as high as a kite on pethidine. Doctors and nurses were fussing round me and trying to decide whether or not to remove my appendix. In the end, they decided not to, and kept me under observation for a few days. Hannah and Tina came to see me, together and separately, and one or two work colleagues came in too. Tina was walking with a stick and looked awful. Apparently, she had fallen over at home. Little Leo came in to see me too. He clung on to me really hard, and I wondered why. Then I remembered, the only other person that he knew who had gone into hospital had never come out alive. The poor little lad probably thought that I was going to die.

Fortunately for me, the suspected appendicitis went away, and I still have my appendix as I write this, eighteen years later. Sarah, my counsellor, was a great believer is stress-related illness, and she maintained that the attack had been my body's way of giving me a few days' rest.

When I came out of hospital, I set myself the goal of going on holiday within a year of leaving Tina. I also resolved to control the amount of overtime I did at work and to try and have some sort of meaningful life outside of work. I wasn't yet sure what shape that was going to take – I knew that I didn't want to be exactly the same person as I had been before I met Tina, but I knew that he hadn't been altogether a bad person.

Printed in Great Britain
by Amazon

57216541R00216